Stand Out 5

Standards-Based English

First Edition

Staci Johnson

Rob Jenkins

HEINLE
CENGAGE Learning

Australia · Brazil · Japan · Korea · Mexico · Singapore · Spain · United Kingdom · United States

HEINLE
CENGAGE Learning™

Stand Out 5: Standards-Based English
Staci Johnson and Rob Jenkins

Publisher: Sherrise Roehr

Acquisitions Editor: Tom Jefferies

Development Editor: Michael Ryall

Director of Content and
Media Production: Michael Burggren

Product Marketing Manager: Katie Kelley

Sr. Content Project Manager: Maryellen E. Killeen

Sr. Print Buyer: Mary Beth Hennebury

Development Editor: Sarah Barnicle

Project Manager: Tunde A. Dewey

Cover / Text Designer: Studio Montage

Photo Researcher: Erika Hokanson

Illustrators: James Edwards, Scott McNeill,
S.I. International

Compositor: PrePressPMG

For product information and technology assistance, contact us at
Cengage Learning Customer & Sales Support, 1-800-354-9706

For permission to use material from this text or product,
submit all requests online at **cengage.com/permissions**
Further permissions questions can be emailed to
permissionrequest@cengage.com

Library of Congress Control Number: 2008933518

ISBN-13: 978-1-4240-1781-2

ISBN-10: 1-4240-1781-5

ISE-10: 1-4240-1909-5

ISE-13: 978-1-4240-1909-0

Cengage Learning
25 Thomson Place
Boston, MA 02210
USA

Cengage Learning is a leading provider of customized learning solutions with office locations around the globe, including Singapore, the United Kingdom, Australia, Mexico, Brazil, and Japan. Locate your local office at:
international.cengage.com/region

Cengage Learning products are represented in Canada by Nelson Education, Ltd.

Visit Heinle online at **elt.heinle.com**
Visit our corporate website at **cengage.com**

Printed in Canada.
1 2 3 4 5 6 7 11 10 09 08

ACKNOWLEDGMENTS

Elizabeth Aderman
*New York City Board of Education,
New York, NY*

Lisa Aago
Fresno Adult School, Fresno, CA

Sharon Baker
Roseville Adult School, Roseville, CA

Lillian Barredo
Stockton School for Adults, Stockton, CA

Linda Boice
*Elk Grove Adult Education,
Elk Grove, CA*

Chan Bostwick
*North Hollywood Polytechnic
Community Adult School,
Sun Valley, CA*

Debra Brooks
*Manhattan BEGIN Program,
New York, NY*

Anne Byrnes
*North Hollywood-Polytechnic
Community Adult School,
Sun Valley, CA*

Rose Cantu
John Jay High School, San Antonio, TX

Toni Chapralis
*Fremont School for Adults,
Sacramento, CA*

Melanie Chitwood
Miami-Dade College, Miami, FL

Geri Creamer
Stockton School for Adults, Stockton, CA

Stephanie Daubar
*Harry W. Brewster Technical Center,
Tampa, FL*

Marie Day
*McHenry County College,
Crystal Lake, IL*

Irene Dennis
San Antonio College, San Antonio, TX

Eileen Duffell
P.S. 64, New York, NY

Nancy Dunlap
*Northside Independent School District,
San Antonio, TX*

Gloria Eriksson
Grant Skills Center, Sacramento, CA

Marti Estrin
*Santa Rosa Junior College,
Santa Rosa, CA*

Lawrence Fish
*Shorefront YM-YWHA English
Language Program, Brooklyn, NY*

Victoria Florit
Miami-Dade College, Miami, FL

Sally Gearheart
*Santa Rosa Junior College,
Santa Rosa, CA*

Rhoda Gilbert
*New York City Board of Education,
New York, NY*

Debbie Glass
Merced Adult School, Merced, CA

Laurie Hartwick
*Lawrence High School/Adult Learning
Center, Lawrence, MA*

Kathleen Jimenez
Miami-Dade College, Miami, FL

Nancy Jordan
*John Jay High School Adult Education,
San Antonio, TX*

Renee Klosz
*Lindsey Hopkins Technical Education
Center, Miami, FL*

David Lauter
Stockton School for Adults, Stockton, CA

Patricia Long
*Old Marshall Adult Education Center,
Sacramento, CA*

Daniel Loos
Seattle Community College, Seattle, WA

Maria Miranda
*Lindsey Hopkins Technical Education
Center, Miami, FL*

Karen Moore
*Stockton School for Adults,
Stockton, CA*

George Myskiw
Malcolm X College, Chicago, IL

Dr. Betty Payne
Montgomery College, Rockville, MD

Adam Pang
*McKinley Community School for
Adults, Honolulu, HI*

Heidi Perez
*Lawrence Public Schools Adult
Learning Center, Lawrence, MA*

Marta Pitt
*Lindsey Hopkins Technical Education
Center, Miami, FL*

Sylvia Rambach
*Stockton School for Adults,
Stockton, CA*

Esther Robbins
*Prince George's Community College,
Largo, MD*

Eric Rosenbaum
*BEGIN Managed Programs,
New York, NY*

Laura Rowley
*Old Marshall Adult Education Center,
Sacramento, CA*

Stephanie Schmitter
*Mercer County Community College,
Trenton, NJ*

Amy Schneider
Pacoima Skills Center, Pacoima, CA

Sr. M. B. Theresa Spittle
Stockton School for Adults, Stockton, CA

Andre Sutton
Belmont Adult School, Los Angeles, CA

Jennifer Swoyer
*Northside Independent School District,
San Antonio, TX*

Marcia Takacs
*Coastline Community College,
Fountain Vallyey, CA*

Claire Valier
*Palm Beach County School District,
West Palm Beach, FL*

Sarah Young
*Arlington Education and Employment
Program (REEP), Arlington, VA*

Staci Johnson

Rob Jenkins

Ever since I can remember, I've been fascinated with other cultures and languages. I love to travel and every place I go, the first thing I want to do is meet the people, learn their language, and understand their culture. Becoming an ESL teacher was a perfect way to turn what I love to do into my profession. There's nothing more incredible than the exchange of teaching and learning from one another that goes on in an ESL classroom. And there's nothing more rewarding than helping a student succeed.

I love teaching. I love to see the expressions on my students' faces when the light goes on and their eyes show such sincere joy of learning. I knew the first time I stepped into an ESL classroom that this was where I needed to be and I have never questioned that resolution. I have worked in business, sales, and publishing, and I've found challenge in all, but nothing can compare to the satisfaction of reaching people in such a personal way.

We are so happy that instructors and agencies have embraced the lesson planning and project-based activities that we introduced in the first edition and are so enthusiastically teaching with **Stand Out**. It is fantastic that so many of our colleagues are as excited to be in this profession as we are. After writing over 500 lesson plans and implementing them in our own classrooms and after personal discussions with thousands of instructors all over the United States and in different parts of the world, we have found ourselves in a position to improve upon our successful model. One of the most notable things in the new edition is that we have continued to stress integrating skills in each lesson and have made this integration more apparent and obvious. To accomplish any life skill, students need to incorporate a combination of reading, writing, listening, speaking, grammar, pronunciation, and academic skills while developing vocabulary and these skills should be taught together in a lesson! We have accomplished this by extending the presentation of lessons in the book, so each lesson is more fully developed. You will also notice an extended list of ancillaries and a tighter correlation of these ancillaries to each book. The ancillaries allow you to extend practice on particular skill areas beyond the lesson in the text. We are so excited about this curriculum and know that as you implement it, you and your students will *stand out*.

Our goal is to give students challenging opportunities to be successful in their language-learning experience so they develop confidence and become independent, lifelong learners.

Staci Johnson
Rob Jenkins

ABOUT THE SERIES

The **Stand Out** series is designed to facilitate *active* learning while challenging students to build a nurturing and effective learning community.

The student books are divided into eight distinct units, mirroring competency areas most useful to newcomers. These areas are outlined in CASAS assessment programs and different state model standards for adults. Each unit in *Stand Out 5* is then divided into five lessons, a review, a research assignment, and a team project. Lessons are driven by performance objectives and are filled with challenging activities that progress from teacher-presented to student-centered tasks.

SUPPLEMENTAL MATERIALS

- The *Stand Out 5 Lesson Planner* is in full color with 60 complete lesson plans, taking the instructor through each stage of a lesson from warm-up and review through application.

- The *Stand Out 5 Activity Bank CD-ROM* has an abundance of customizable worksheets. Print or download and modify what you need for your particular class.

- The *Stand Out 5 Grammar Challenge* is a workbook that gives additional grammar explanation and practice in context.

- The *Stand Out 5 Assessment CD-ROM with ExamView®* allows you to customize pre- and post-tests for each unit as well as a pre- and post-test for the book.

- Listening scripts are found in the back of the student book and in the Lesson Planner. CDs are available with focused listening activities described in the Lesson Planner.

STAND OUT 5 LESSON PLANNER

The *Stand Out 5 Lesson Planner* is a new and innovative approach. As many seasoned teachers know, good lesson planning can make a substantial difference in the classroom. Students continue coming to class, understanding, applying, and remembering more of what they learn. They are more confident in their learning when good lesson planning techniques are incorporated.

We have developed lesson plans that are designed to be used each day and to reduce preparation time. The planner includes:

- Standard lesson progression (Warm-up and Review, Introduction, Presentation, Practice, Evaluation, and Application)

- A creative and complete way to approach varied class lengths so that each lesson will work within a class period.

- 180 hours of classroom activities
- Time suggestions for each activity
- Pedagogical comments
- Space for teacher notes and future planning
- Identification of LCP standards in addition to SCANS and CASAS standards

USER QUESTIONS ABOUT STAND OUT

- **What are SCANS and EFF and how do they integrate into the book?**
  SCANS is the Secretary's Commission on Achieving Necessary Skills. SCANS was developed to encourage students to prepare for the workplace. The standards developed through SCANS have been incorporated throughout the **Stand Out** student books and components.

  Stand Out addresses SCANS a little differently than do other books. SCANS standards elicit effective teaching strategies by incorporating essential skills such as critical thinking and group work. We have incorporated SCANS standards in every lesson, not isolating these standards in the work unit. All new texts have followed our lead.

  EFF, or **E**quipped **F**or the **F**uture, is another set of standards established to address students' roles as parents, workers, and citizens, with a vision of student literacy and lifelong learning. **Stand Out** addresses these standards and integrates them into the materials in a similar way to SCANS.

- **What about CASAS?** The federal government has mandated that states show student outcomes as a prerequisite to receiving funding. Some states have incorporated the **C**omprehensive **A**dult **S**tudent **A**ssessment **S**ystem (CASAS) testing to standardize agency reporting. Unfortunately, many of our students are unfamiliar with standardized testing and therefore struggle with it. Adult schools need to develop lesson plans to address specific concerns. **Stand Out** was developed with careful attention to CASAS skill areas in most lessons and performance objectives.

- **Are the tasks too challenging for my students?**
  Students learn by doing and learn more when challenged. **Stand Out** provides tasks that encourage critical thinking in a variety of ways. The tasks in each lesson move from teacher-directed to student-centered so the learner clearly understands what's expected and is willing to "take a risk." The lessons are expected to be challenging. In this way, students learn that when they work together as a learning community, anything becomes possible. The satisfaction of accomplishing something both as an

individual and as a member of a team results in greater confidence and effective learning.

- **Do I need to understand lesson planning to teach from the student book?** If you don't understand lesson planning when you start, you will when you finish! Teaching from **Stand Out** is like a course on lesson planning, especially if you use the Lesson Planner on a daily basis.

  Stand Out does *stand out* because, when we developed this series, we first established performance objectives for each lesson. Then we designed lesson plans, followed by student book pages. The introduction to each lesson varies because different objectives demand different approaches. **Stand Out's** variety of tasks makes learning more interesting for the student.

- **What is the research project?** The purpose of each research project is to empower students to seek information on the Internet, in other publications, and in their community. The resulting information will provide students with helpful and practical sources for independent research after the course.

- **What are team projects?** The final lesson of each unit is a **team project**. This is often a team simulation that incorporates the objectives of the unit and provides an additional opportunity for students to actively apply what they have learned. The project allows students to produce something that represents their progress in learning. These end-of-unit projects were created with a variety of learning styles and individual skills in mind. The team projects can be skipped or simplified, but we encourage instructors to implement them, enriching the overall student experience.

- **What do you mean by a customizable Activity Bank?** Every class, student, teacher, and approach is different. Since no one textbook can meet all these differences, the *Stand Out Activity Bank CD-ROM* allows you to customize **Stand Out** for your class. You can copy different activities and worksheets from the CD-ROM to your hard drive and then:

  - change items in supplemental vocabulary, grammar, and life skill activities;

  - personalize activities with student names and popular locations in your area;

  - extend every lesson with additional practice where you feel it is most needed.

  The Activity Bank also includes the following resources:

  - Multilevel worksheets – worksheets based on the standard worksheets described above, but at one level higher and one level lower.

- Graphic organizer templates – templates that can be used to facilitate learning. They include graphs, charts, VENN diagrams, and so on.

- Computer worksheets – worksheets designed to supplement each unit and progress from simple to complex operations in word processing; and spreadsheets for labs and computer enhanced classrooms.

- Internet worksheets – worksheets designed to supplement each unit and provide application opportunities beyond the lessons in the book.

- **Is *Stand Out* grammar-based or competency-based?** **Stand Out** is a competency-based series; however, students are exposed to basic grammar structures. We believe that grammar instruction in context is extremely important. Grammar is a necessary component for achieving most competencies; therefore it is integrated into most lessons. Students are first provided with context that incorporates the grammar, followed by an explanation and practice. At this level, we expect students to learn basic structures, but we do not expect them to acquire them. It has been our experience that students are exposed several times within their learning experience to language structures before they actually acquire them. For teachers who want to enhance grammar instruction, the *Activity Bank CD-ROM* and/or the *Grammar Challenge* workbooks provide ample opportunities.

  The six competencies that drive **Stand Out** are communication, consumer economics, community resources, health, occupational knowledge, and lifelong learning (civic responsibility replaces lifelong learning in Book 5).

- **Are there enough activities so I don't have to supplement?** **Stand Out** stands alone in providing 180 hours of instruction and activities, even without the additional suggestions in the Lesson Planner. The Lesson Planner also shows you how to streamline lessons to provide 90 hours of classwork and still have thorough lessons if you meet less often. When supplementing with the *Stand Out Activity Bank CD-ROM*, the *Assessment CD-ROM with ExamView®* and the *Stand Out Grammar Challenge* workbook, you gain unlimited opportunities to extend class hours and provide activities related directly to each lesson objective. Calculate how many hours your class meets in a semester and look to **Stand Out** to address the full class experience.

  Stand Out is a comprehensive approach to adult language learning, meeting needs of students and instructors completely and effectively.

● Grammar points that are new △ Grammar points that are being recycled ◆ Grammar points that are presented in context

	Numeracy/ Academic Strategies	EFF	SCANS	CASAS
Pre-Unit	• Pronunciation: Enunciate clearly • Develop research skills and ideas • Take notes • Focused listening • Prepare and deliver an oral presentation • Write a personal letter/e-mail	Many EFF skills are incorporated into this unit with an emphasis on: **Communication:** • Conveying ideas in writing • Speaking so others can understand • Listening actively **Lifelong Learning:** • Learning through reasearch • Taking responsibility for learning	Many SCANS skills are incorporated in this unit with an emphasis on: • Listening • Speaking • Social • Visualization • Cultural diversity	**1:** 0.1.1, 0.1.2, 0.1.4, 7.2.1 **2:** 0.2.1, 0.2.4 **3:** 0.2.3 **RE:** 7.44
Unit 1	• Reading • Interpret meanings of words in context • Develop categories • Write a paragraph • Focused listening • Take notes from lecture/oral sources • Interpret bar graphs • Research online	Many EFF skills are incorporated into this unit with an emphasis on: **Communication:** • Reading with understanding • Observing critically **Decision-Making:** • Planning **Lifelong Learning:** • Using information and communications technololgy • Learning through research	Many SCANS skills are incorporated in this unit with an emphasis on: • Writing • Social • Negotiation • Leadership • Self-esteem • Self-management • Responsibility • Decision making	**VB:** 7.4.5 **1:** 7.4.2, 7.4.9 **2:** 4.1.9, 7.4.2 **3:** 7.4.2 **4:** 7.1.1, 7.1.2, 7.1.3, 7.4.2 **5:** 7.1.3 **RV:** 7.2.1 **RE:** 4.9.3, 7.2.1, 7.4.4, 7.4.5, 7.4.6 **TP:** 4.8.1, 4.8.5, 4.8.6
Unit 2	• Interpret meaning of idioms in context • Focused listening • Analyze and evaluate readings and budgets • Outline readings • Summarize reading passages and other sources of information • Make calculations • Create a budget	Many EFF skills are incorporated into this unit with an emphasis on: **Communication:** • Observing critically **Decision-Making:** • Using math to solve problems and communicate • Solving problems and making decisions • Planning **Lifelong Learning:** • Using information and communications technololgy • Learning through research • Reflecting and evaluating	Many SCANS skills are incorporated in this unit with an emphasis on: • Mathematics • Social • Self-management • Responsibility • Problem-solving • Decision making	**VB:** 7.4.5 **1:** 1.5.1, 4.1.4, 2.5.5 **2:** 1.6.2 **3:** 7.4.2 **4:** 1.3.2, 7.4.2 **5:** 1.6.2, 7.4.2 **RV:** 7.2.1 **RE:** 4.9.3, 7.2.1, 7.4.4, 7.4.5, 7.4.6 **TP:** 4.8.1, 4.8.5, 4.8.6

Contents

CONTENTS

● Grammar points that are new   △ Grammar points that are being recycled   ◆ Grammar points that are presented in context

Numeracy/ Academic Skills	EFF	SCANS	CASAS
Unit 3 • Organize sentences effectively to convey meaning • Focused listening • Read and interpret information • Scan for details • Outline prior to writing • Write two paragraph essay • Research through interview and on the computer • Make calculations • Interpret a chart	Many EFF skills are incorporated into this unit with an emphasis on: **Communication:** • Observing critically **Decision-Making:** • Using math to solve problems and communicate • Solving problems and making decisions • Planning **Lifelong Learning:** • Using information and communications technolololgy • Learning through research • Reflecting and evaluating	Many SCANS skills are incorporated in this unit with an emphasis on: • Mathematics • Reading • Writing • Listening • Negotiation • Decision making	VB: 7.4.5 **1:** 1.9.5 **2:** 1.9.6 **3:** 1.9.8 **4:** 1.9.3 **5:** 1.9.2 RV:7.2.1 RE:4.9.3, 7.2.1, 7.4.4, 7.4.5, 7.4.6 TP:4.8.1, 4.8.5, 4.8.6
Unit 4 • Understand and use parts of speech related to root words • Focused listening • Summarize reading passages • Scan for details • Skim for general ideas • Prepare and deliver an oral presentation • Research online	Many EFF skills are incorporated into this unit with an emphasis on: **Communication:** • Reading with understanding **Decision-Making:** • Solving problems and making decisions • Resolving conflict and negotiating • Cooperating with others **Lifelong Learning:** • Learning through research • Reflecting and evaluating	Many SCANS skills are incorporated in this unit with an emphasis on: • Problem-solving • Self-management • Reading • Mathematics • Creative thinking • Responsibility • Visualization	VB:7.4.5 **1:** 2.1.8 **2:** 1.4.3 **3:** 1.4.5 **4:** 1.4.6 **5:** 1.4.7, 1.4.8 RV:7.2.1 RE:4.9.3, 7.2.1, 7.4.4, 7.4.5, 7.4.6 TP:4.8.1, 4.8.5, 4.8.6
Unit 5 • Analyze and use root words and related parts of speech • Focused listening • Make calculations • Interview others • Understand bar graphs • Read a spread sheet • Brainstorm • Use reference materials including a computer	Many EFF skills are incorporated into this unit with an emphasis on: **Communication:** • Listening actively • Observing critically **Decision-Making:** • Using math to solve problems and communicate • Solving problems and making decisions • Resolving conflict and negotiating • Cooperating with others **Lifelong Learning:** • Using information and communications technology	Many SCANS skills are incorporated in this unit with an emphasis on: • Mathematics • Reading • Self-esteem • Self-management • Responsibility • Problem-solving • Visualization • Decision making	VB:7.4.5 **1:** 3.5.8, 3.5.9 **2:** 3.2.3, 3.2.4 **3:** 3.2.3, 3.4.5 **4:** 3.2.3 **5:** 3.4.3 RV:7.2.1 RE:4.9.3, 7.2.1, 7.4.4, 7.4.5, 7.4.6 TP:4.8.1, 4.8.5, 4.8.6

• Grammar points that are new   △ Grammar points that are being recycled   ◆ Grammar points that are presented in context

Numeracy/ Academic Skills	EFF	SCANS	CASAS
Unit 6 • Understand and use synonyms • Use reference materials • Research online • Use a computer to study • Take notes • Scan for main ideas and details • Brainstorm and construct arguments	**Many EFF skills are incorporated into this unit with an emphasis on:** **Communication:** • Reading with understanding • Speaking so others can understand • Listening actively **Decision-Making:** • Solving problems and making decisions • Resolving conflict and negotiating • Advocating and influencing • Cooperating with others **Lifelong Learning:** • Learning through research	**Many SCANS skills are incorporated in this unit with an emphasis on:** • Social interaction • Negotiation • Self-management • Decision making • Writing	VB:7.4.5 **1:** 1.2.4, 1.2.3, 1.2.5, 6.4.1, 6.4.3, 7.4.4 **2:** 1.3.1, 1.3.3 **3:** 1.6.3, 1.6.4, 1.7.1 **4:** 1.3.3 **5:** 1.6.3 RV:7.2.1 RE:4.9.3, 7.2.1, 7.4.4, 7.4.5, 7.4.6 TP:4.8.1, 4.8.5, 4.8.6
Unit 7 • Interpret visual representations • Understand root words and suffixes • Analyze and evaluate • Understand and write directions and reports • Focused listening • Summarize reading passages	**Many EFF skills are incorporated into this unit with an emphasis on:** **Communication:** • Reading with understanding • Conveying ideas in writing **Decision-Making:** • Solving problems and making decisions **Lifelong Learning:** • Using information and communications technololgy • Learning through research • Reflecting and evaluating	**Many SCANS skills are incorporated in this unit with an emphasis on:** • Social • Problem-solving • Visualization • Creative thinking • Negotiation • Teamwork • Leadership • Reading	VB:4.5.1, 7.4.5 **1:** 4.4.8, 4.5.1, 4.5.4, 4.5.6 **2:** 4.5.7 **3:** 4.5.3, 4.7.2 **4:** 4.8.1, 4.8.5, 4.8.6 **5:** 4.6.4 RV:7.2.1 RE:4.9.3, 7.2.1, 7.4.4, 7.4.5, 7.4.6 TP:4.8.1, 4.8.5, 4.8.6
Unit 8 • Interpret meanings of words in context • Focused listening • Scan for details • Skim for general ideas • Identify and paraphrase information • Analyze and evaluate • Interview others • Write a paragraph • Use transitional expressions in writing • Create visual representation to brainstorm • Write a speech	**Many EFF skills are incorporated into this unit with an emphasis on:** **Communication:** • Reading with understanding • Conveying ideas in writing • Speaking so others can understand • Listening actively **Decision-Making:** • Advocating and influencing • Cooperating with others **Lifelong Learning:** • Learning through research • Reflecting and evaluating • Taking responsibility for learning	**Many SCANS skills are incorporated in this unit with an emphasis on:** • Reading • Speaking • Responsibility • Cultural diversity • Decision making	VB:7.4.5 **1:** 1.5.1, 5.3.6 **2:** 1.6.2, 5.2.2, 5.3.2, 5.7.1, **3:** 5.6.2 , 5.3.8, 7.4.2 **4:** 1.3.2, 5.3.7, 5.7.1, 7.4.2 **5:** 5.1.6, 5.7.1, 7.4.2 R: 7.2.1 RE:4.9.3, 7.2.1, 7.4.4, 7.4.5, 7.4.6 IP: 4.8.1, 4.8.5, 4.8.6

Contents

Welcome to Stand Out

Stand Out works.

And now it works even better!

Built from the standards necessary for adult English learners, *Stand Out* gives students the foundation and tools they need to develop confidence and become independent, lifelong learners.

- State and federally required **life skills and competencies** are taught, helping students meet necessary benchmarks.

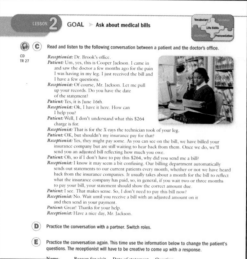

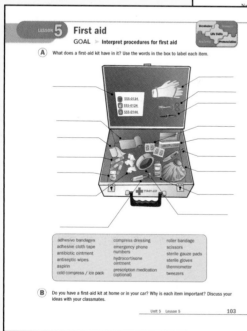

- Key **vocabulary** is introduced visually and orally.

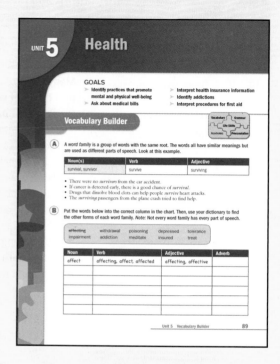

- Clearly defined **goals** provide a roadmap of learning for the student.
- **New to Level 5!** The Vocabulary Builder provides two full pages of exercises designed to draw out student knowledge of vocabulary and practice vocabulary used in each unit.

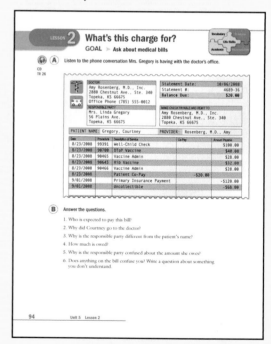

- A variety of **examples from real life**, like bills, insurance documents, contracts, newspaper ads, maps, etc. help students learn to access information and resources in their community.

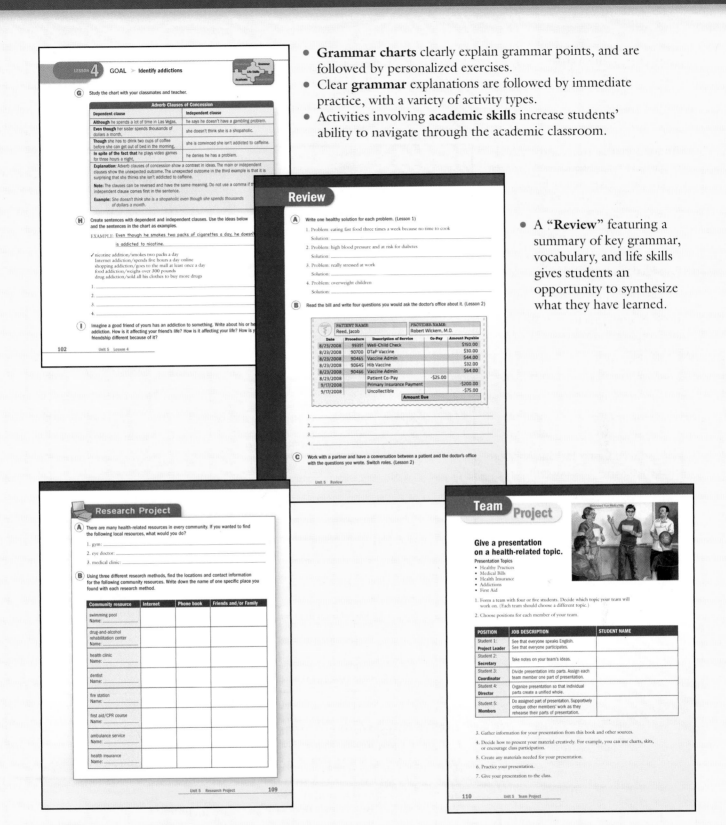

- **Grammar charts** clearly explain grammar points, and are followed by personalized exercises.
- Clear **grammar** explanations are followed by immediate practice, with a variety of activity types.
- Activities involving **academic skills** increase students' ability to navigate through the academic classroom.

- A **"Review"** featuring a summary of key grammar, vocabulary, and life skills gives students an opportunity to synthesize what they have learned.

- A **"Research Project"** at the end of each unit helps students become more competent at the academic skills needed for computer and library research.
- The **"Student Goals" Checklist** in the endmatter provides opportunities for learner self-assessment.

- **"Team Projects"** present motivating cross-ability activities which group learners of different levels together to complete a task that applies the unit objective.

The ground-breaking *Stand Out* **Lesson Planners** take the guesswork out of meeting the standards while offering high-interest, meaningful language activities, and three levels of pacing for each book.

- An **at-a-glance prep** and **agenda section** for each lesson ensure that instructors have a clear knowledge of what will be covered in the lesson.

- A complete **lesson plan** for each page in the student book is provided, following a standard lesson progression (Warm-up and Review, Introduction, Presentation, Practice, Evaluation, and Application).

- Clear, easy-to-identify **pacing guide** icons offer three different pacing strategies.

- **"Teaching Tips"** provide ideas and strategies for the classroom.

- **"Standards Correlations"** appear directly on the page, detailing how *Stand Out* meets CASAS, EFF, and SCANS standards.

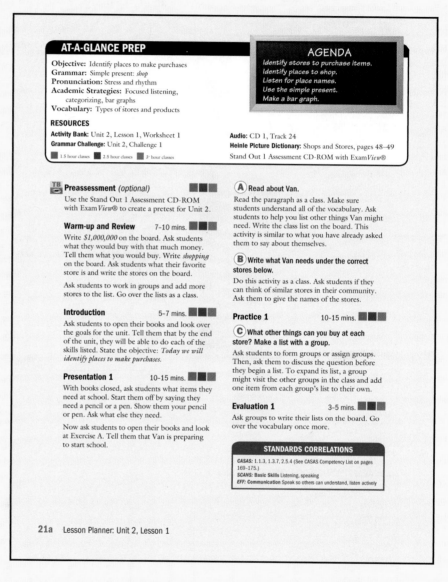

- Additional **supplemental activities** found on the *Activity Bank CD-ROM* are suggested at their point of use.
- The *Activity Bank CD-ROM* includes **reproducible multilevel activity masters** for each lesson that can be printed or downloaded and modified for classroom needs.
- **"Listening Scripts"** from the *Audio CD* are included.

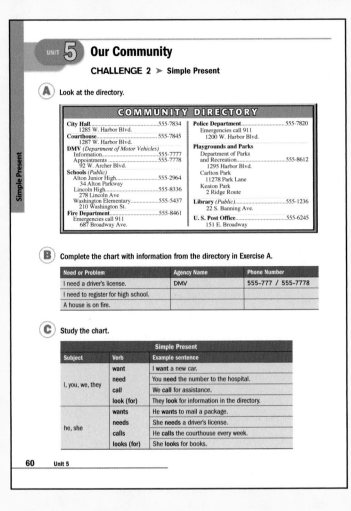

UNIT 5 — Our Community

CHALLENGE 2 ➤ Simple Present

(A) Look at the directory.

COMMUNITY DIRECTORY

City Hall..................555-7834 1285 W. Harbor Blvd.	**Police Department**.....................555-7820 Emergencies call 911 1200 W. Harbor Blvd.
Courthouse..................555-7845 1287 W. Harbor Blvd.	
DMV *(Department of Motor Vehicles)* Information............................555-7777 Appointments........................555-7778 92 W. Archer Blvd.	**Playgrounds and Parks** Department of Parks and Recreation.................555-8612 1295 Harbor Blvd.
Schools *(Public)* Alton Junior High.................555-2964 34 Alton Parkway Lincoln High.........................555-8336 278 Lincoln Ave Washington Elementary.......555-5437 210 Washington St.	Carlton Park 11278 Park Lane Keaton Park 2 Ridge Route
	Library *(Public)*...............555-1236 22 S. Banning Ave.
Fire Department...............555-8461 Emergencies call 911 687 Broadway Ave.	**U. S. Post Office**......................555-6245 151 E. Broadway

(B) Complete the chart with information from the directory in Exercise A.

Need or Problem	Agency Name	Phone Number
I need a driver's license.	DMV	555-777 / 555-7778
I need to register for high school.		
A house is on fire.		

(C) Study the chart.

Simple Present		
Subject	**Verb**	**Example sentence**
I, you, we, they	want	I want a new car.
	need	You need the number to the hospital.
	call	We call for assistance.
	look (for)	They look for information in the directory.
he, she	wants	He wants to mail a package.
	needs	She needs a driver's license.
	calls	He calls the courthouse every week.
	looks (for)	She looks for books.

- A variety of **activities** allow students develop their grammar skills and apply them.
- Written by **Rob Jenkins** and **Staci Johnson**, the *Grammar Challenge* workbooks are directly aligned to the student books.

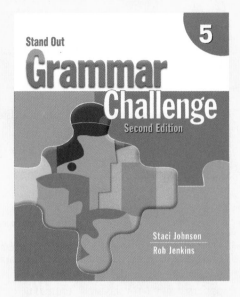

Stand Out

Grammar Challenge
Second Edition

Staci Johnson
Rob Jenkins

- *Grammar Challenge* workbooks include supplemental activities for students who desire even more contextual grammar and vocabulary practice.
- Clear and concise **grammar explanation boxes** provide a strong foundation for the activities.

(D) Complete the sentences with the correct form of the verb in the simple present.

1. Kenji _____ (need) the police immediately.
2. The women _____ (call) the hospital every hour.
3. He _____ (want) to mail a package to his mother in Columbia.
4. She _____ (look) for places to have a picnic in the city directory.
5. We _____ (call) the DMV when we buy a new car.
6. I _____ (like) the doctor on Main Street.
7. She _____ (prefer) to go to a park.
8. The nurse _____ (call) the doctor every day.
9. We _____ (eat) lunch at the restaurant on the corner.
10. The bus _____ (stops) on the corner of Main and Nutwood.
11. I _____ (visit) Marie on Saturdays.
12. My husband _____ (come) with me to the hospital.

(E) Write reasons why Raquel may call. What do you think?

1. (bank) Raquel needs money.
2. (dentist) Raquel
3. (shoe store) Raquel
4. (doctors) Raquel and Marie
5. (optometrist) Raquel
6. (hospital) Raquel and Mario
7. (DMV) Raquel
8. (fire department) Mario

(F) Write reasons why you may call a restaurant, a bank, and a rental car agency.

1. (restaurant) _____
2. (market) _____
3. (rental car agency) _____

Text Credits

Pre-Unit
Page P10 Source: *Heinle Newbury House Dictionary of American English*, 4th edition

Unit 1
Page 7 "Educational Attainment and Earning Power for Men and Women 18 and Over" chart.
Source: U.S. Census Bureau, Current Population Survey 2006. Annual Social and Economic Supplement.

Unit 2
Page 34 "The Four Keys to Great Credit" is used by permission. Liz Pulliam Weston is a personal finance columnist for **MSN Money** (Web site source: http://money.msn.com), where this article first appeared. Her column appears every Monday and Thursday, exclusively on *MSN Money*. She also answers reader questions in the Your Money message board.

Unit 3
Page 60 "Occupant Fatalities in 2004 by Age and Restraint Use in Passenger Vehicles"
Web site source: http://www.nhtsa.dot.gov
Page 61 "Facts on alcohol-related accidents"
Web site source: http://www.cdc.gov/ncipc/factsheets/drving.htm

Unit 4
Page 82 "Theft Prevention Newsletter" Web site source: http://www.jcsd.org/burglary_prevention.htm

Unit 5
Page 97 "Percentage of persons without health insurance, by three measurements and age group, and percentage of persons with health insurance, by coverage type and age group: United States, January, 2007–June, 2007" Source: Family Core component of the 2007 National Health Interview Survey. The estimates for 2007 are based on data collected January through June. Data are based on household interviews of a sample of the civilian non-institutionalized population.
Page 98 "Percentage of persons under 65 years of age without health insurance coverage at the time of interview, by age group and sex: United States, January, 2007–June, 2007"

Source: Family Core component of the 2007 National Health Interview Survey. The estimates for 2007 are based on data collected January through June. Data are based on household interviews of a sample of the civilian non-institutionalized population.

Page 99 "Percentage of persons who lacked health insurance coverage at the time of interview, for at least part of the past year, or for more than a year, by selected demographic characteristics: United States, January, 2007–June, 2007."
Source: Family Core component of the 2007 National Health Interview Survey. The estimates for 2007 are based on data collected in January through June. Data are based on household interviews of a sample of the civilian non-institutionalized population.

Page 107 "Health Insurance Coverage of Adults 19–64 Living in Poverty, New York State (2005–2006)" Sources: Urban Institute and Kaiser Commission on Medicaid and the Uninsured estimates based on the Census Bureau's March 2006 and 2007 Current Population Survey (CPS: Annual Social and Economic Supplements). Web site source: http://www.statehealthfacts.org/comparebar.jsp?ind=131&cat=3

Unit 7
Page 143-146 "Conflict Resolution: Resolving Conflict Rationally and Effectively" Used with permission from ©Mind Tools Ltd, 1995–2008. All Rights Reserved.
Page 147 Progress report guidelines. Reprinted with permission from David A. McMurrey, author of *Power Tools for Technical Communication*, Boston: Heinle, 2001.

Unit 8
Page 158 U.S. Citizenship and Immigration Services, Web site source: www.uscis.gov
Page 163 "The Mothers' Club of Northville" Reprinted by permission of the City of Northville, MI.
Web site source: http://www.ci.northville.mi.us
Page 166 "Create Less Trash" and "In Your Home—Conserve Energy" Used with permission from Sustainable Environment for Quality of Life,
Web site source: www.seql.org
Page 167 "Carpooling—What is it?" Used with permission from Sustainable Environment for Quality of Life,
Web site source: www.seql.org

Getting to Know You

GOALS

➤ **Get to know your classmates**

➤ **Talk about personal interests**

➤ **Write a personal letter**

LESSON **1**

Classroom community

GOAL ➤ **Get to know your classmates**

CD
TR 1

(A) Read and listen to the conversation between Liam and Rani. Do you know people like them?

(B) Using the conversation in Exercise A as an example, introduce yourself to four classmates.

(C) Who are the four classmates you met? Write their names, where they are from, and something interesting you learned about them in the chart below.

Name	Country	Interesting fact

GOAL ➤ **Get to know your classmates**

 CD TR 2

D Read and listen to the conversation between Liam, Rani, and Haru. What does Liam say to introduce Haru to Rani?

Rani, I'd like you to meet Haru. He is from Japan and came here last year.

It's a pleasure to meet you, Haru. You seem very young!

Actually, I just finished high school, but my English writing still isn't good enough to go to college, so I'm going to study for one more year before I apply.

Oh, that's smart. You remind me of my son. We came here when he was in high school, too.

E Study the expressions below.

Introduction	Responding to an introduction
I'd like to introduce you to _____.	(It's) A pleasure . . . to meet you.
I'd like you to meet _____.	. . . meeting you.
This is (friend's name) _____.	(I'm) Pleased to meet you.
Do you know _____?	(It's) Nice to meet you.
Have you met _____?	(It's) Good to meet you.

F Pair up with one of the classmates you have met. Introduce this person to four people in your class. Make sure you include the person's name, country, and an interesting fact about him or her in your introduction.

G Read and listen to Haru as he introduces Kimla to the class.

CD
TR 3

Nice to meet you, Kimla.

I'd like you to meet Kimla. She came here with her family from Saudi Arabia four years ago. She has been studying English for three years now and would like to become a registered nurse. She hopes to apply to a nursing program at the end of this semester.

H Choose two people that you have met in class today. Write introductions for them below. Use Haru's introduction in Exercise G as an example.

Name of classmate: _____

Information about classmate: _____

_____

_____

Name of classmate: _____

Information about classmate: _____

_____

_____

I Choose one of the people from Exercise H to introduce to the class.

LESSON 2 — What are your hobbies?

GOAL ➤ Talk about personal interests

A Look at the pictures of Haru, Rani, and Kimla. What do you think their personal interests are? Write them on the lines below the pictures.

_____   _____   _____

_____   _____   _____

CD
TR 4

B Listen to the conversation between Haru, Rani, and Kimla. Then answer the questions below.

1. What kind of video games does Haru like to play? _____

2. What are three types of reading Kimla likes to do? _____

3. What kind of pictures does Rani like to take? _____

4. Where does Haru play his video games? _____

5. What doesn't Haru like to do? _____

6. How late does Kimla stay up reading? _____

7. Who does Haru remind Rani of? _____

8. What gift did Rani's son give her? _____

C Share your answers with a partner.

D People have many different types of interests. Look at the three categories of interests below. Can you think of some examples for each category?

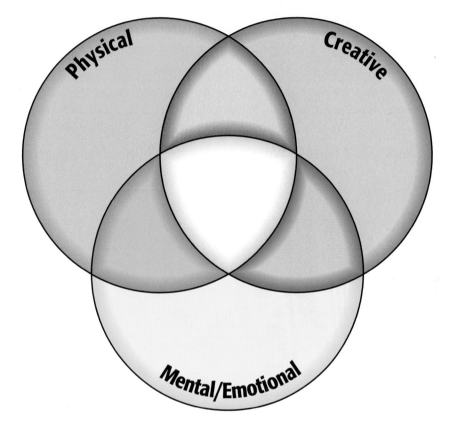

E Working with a small group, put each of the activities below into the circle you think is most appropriate. Some activities may belong in more than one circle.

cook	lift weights	run
do crossword puzzles	paint	swim
do yoga	play soccer	take pictures
draw	play video games	watch movies
knit	read	write

F Now think about your own personal interests. Write them in the appropriate categories.

Physical: _____

Creative: _____

Mental/Emotional: _____

GOAL ➤ **Talk about personal interests**

G How would you ask people about their personal interests? Study the phrases below.

> **Asking about Personal Interests**
> So, what do you like to do in your free time?
> What are your hobbies?
> What are your interests outside of school/work?

H Work with a partner. Write a conversation in which you discuss your personal interests.

A: _____

B: _____

A: _____

B: _____

A: _____

B: _____

A: _____

B: _____

A: _____

B: _____

A: _____

B: _____

A: _____

B: _____

I In a small group, discuss your personal interests. When you have finished, share what you have learned about each other with the rest of the class.

Dear friend

GOAL ➤ **Write a personal letter**

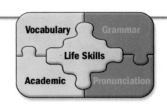

A Read the e-mail message that Liam wrote to his family.

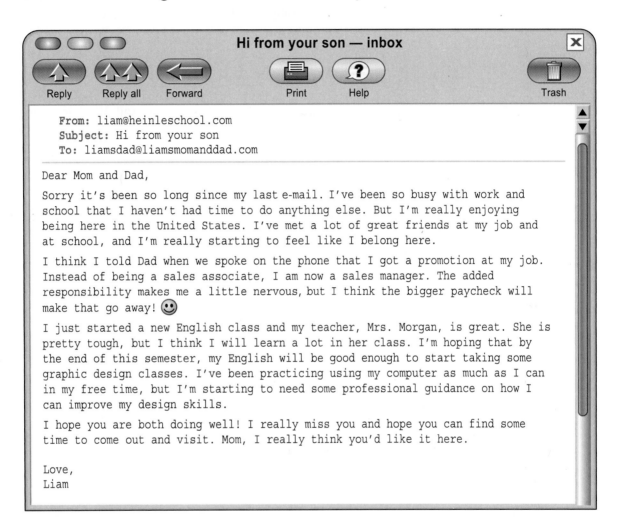

B This is a personal letter, not a formal letter. How can you tell that this letter is personal?

_____

C What do you think the following expressions mean?

1. feel like I belong _____

2. pretty tough _____

3. added responsibility _____

4. professional guidance _____

LESSON 3   **GOAL** ➤ **Write a personal letter**

D   A personal letter is a letter that you write to a family member, a friend, or someone who you already know. Personal letters usually contain personal information and are written informally. Think of some people that you might write a personal letter to. Who are they?

_____

E   There are many reasons for writing a personal letter or e-mail. Work in a small group to come up with a short list.

Reasons for writing a personal letter or e-mail:

1. _____

2. _____

3. _____

4. _____

F   Read Liam's thank-you note. There are nine mistakes. Find the mistakes and correct them.

> *Dear Aunt Claire and Uncle Laurent*
>
> *Thanks you so much for the crystal wine glasses you sent us for our aniversary. They is absolutely beutiful and I cant wait to has a dinner party, so we can show them off. It was so thoughtful of you to think of us on our special day. I hope you are both doing well and we hopes to see you soon!*
>
> *sincerely,*
>
> *Liam*

G   Rewrite Liam's note on a separate piece of paper. Correct the mistakes.

H Mrs. Morgan asked her class to choose someone they had just met in class and send them an e-mail. Read the e-mail that Rani wrote to Kimla.

> ✉ **Nice to meet you!**
>
> File   Edit   View   Isert   Format   Tools   Action   Help   Type a question here
>
> ↺ Reply   ↺ Reply to all   ➡ Forward   🖨 Print   ⬆ ⬇ ⊘ Delete ?
>
> **From:**   Your friend Rani   <rani@heinleschool.com>
> **Subject:** Nice to meet you!
> **To:**   kimla@heinleschool.com
>
> Dear Kimla,
>
> It was so nice to meet you in class the other day. I really enjoyed learning some new things about you. I'd like to tell you a little bit more about myself.
>
> My family came over here from India 20 years ago so that our children could finish up their education here. We wanted to give them as many opportunities as possible, and we had heard such good things about the higher education system in the United States. We have two sons, both of whom are married now with families of their own. I take care of the four grandchildren during the day before and after school.
>
> Someday, when the kids are grown up and don't need me anymore, I would like to take some photography classes. I don't know if I will ever do anything professional with photography, but it is so intriguing to me and I would like to learn more. So that's a little bit about me.
>
> I do hope to know you better as our class goes along. You seem like such a nice young woman, and I hope that we can be friends.
>
> Sincerely,
> Rani

I Now choose one of the classmates you recently met and write this person a personal letter about yourself on a separate piece of paper.

Research Project

Who do you know? What do they know?

A *Research* is defined as "a study of information about something." *To research* something is "to study something deeply." A synonym for the verb *research* is *investigate*.
(Source: *Heinle Newbury House Dictionary of American English*, 4th edition)

At the end of each unit in this book, you will be learning a new research strategy. Why is learning how to conduct research important? Discuss your ideas with your classmates.

B Let's say you want to find out where the best Japanese restaurant is in town. How would you research this topic? Write down your ideas.

_____

C Talking to people is one of the best ways to do research. Talk to your classmates about the following topics. Write down the best ideas you get for each topic.

1. the best place to buy a new computer: _____

_____

2. the closest bank: _____

_____

3. how to find a good babysitter: _____

_____

4. ideas for saving money: _____

_____

Share your research with your classmates.

D What else do you want to know? Think of a topic and then do some research! Remember to ask your classmates for ideas.

What I want to know: _____

My research findings: _____

_____

_____

Balancing Your Life

GOALS
➤ **Identify your learning style**
➤ **Identify a career path**
➤ **Balance your life**

➤ **Identify and prioritize goals**
➤ **Motivate yourself**

Vocabulary Builder

A Read about these students. What can you learn about each person?
Discuss with a small group.

Learning Style:
visual
Career Path:
graphic designer
Motivation:
financial

Liam

Learning Style:
visual
Career Path:
photographer
Motivation:
joy

Rani

Learning Style:
tactile
Career Path:
computer
programmer
Motivation:
fun

Haru

Learning Style:
auditory
Career Path:
registered nurse
Motivation:
time with family

Kimla

B You will study the following ideas in this unit. What do you think each expression means?
Write your own thoughts.

1. Learning style: _____

2. Career path: _____

3. Motivation: _____

Vocabulary Builder

C Below are groups of vocabulary words that you will be working with in this unit. Make your best guess as to which topic goes with each group of phrases. Write the appropriate topic on the line above each group of words.

> **Topics**
>
> Career Path   Learning Styles   Multiple Intelligences
> Goal Setting   Motivation

1. _____
   auditory
   tactile/kinesthetic
   visual

2. _____
   earning power
   pursue
   educational attainment

3. _____
   auditory
   bodily/rhythmic
   interpersonal
   intrapersonal
   logical

4. _____
   naturalistic
   spatial
   verbal/linguistic
   visual
   tactile/kinesthetic

5. _____
   achieve
   balance
   long-term
   motivate
   prioritize
   short-term

6. _____
   be flexible
   evaluate progress
   inspire
   monitor progress
   positive outlook
   support

D Put a check next to each term you are familiar with.

E Choose two new terms from Exercise C that you would like to know the meanings of. Look the items up in a dictionary. Write the word, part of speech, definition, word forms, and the example sentence— if there is one—that you find in each dictionary entry. An example has been done for you.

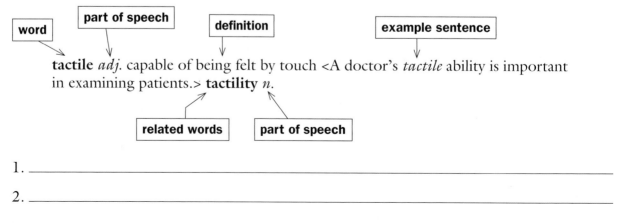

1. _____

2. _____

Learning styles

GOAL ➤ **Identify your learning style**

Vocabulary · Grammar
Life Skills
Academic · Pronunciation

A Think about how you learn new skills and ideas. Do you . . .

☐ learn through seeing?   ☐ learn through listening?   ☐ learn through moving, doing, and touching?

CD
TR 5

B Listen to a lecturer talk about the three learning styles and take notes. Write down any key words you hear to describe each learning style.

Visual	Auditory	Tactile/Kinesthetic
seeing		
body language		
facial expressions		

C Indicate the learning style next to each activity. Write *V* for *Visual*, *A* for *Auditory*, and *T/K* for *Tactile/Kinesthetic* on the line.

1. touching objects _____

2. watching a video _____

3. looking at a diagram _____

4. reading a textbook _____

5. doing a science experiment _____

6. listening to a lecture _____

7. participating in a discussion _____

D Check the learning style you think best describes you.

____ visual   ____ auditory   ____ tactile/kinesthetic

GOAL ➤ **Identify your learning style**

Vocabulary | Grammar
Life Skills
Academic | Pronunciation

E What do you think *intelligence* means? Discuss the term with a partner and write your ideas on the lines below.

_____

_____

Now look the word up in a dictionary. Write its definition below.

intelligence *n* _____

F Read about multiple intelligences. Underline the main idea in each paragraph.

MULTIPLE INTELLIGENCES

According to psychologist Howard Gardner, there are eight different ways to show intellectual ability. These eight intelligences are described as visual/spatial, verbal/linguistic, logical/mathematical, bodily/kinesthetic, musical/rhythmic, interpersonal, intrapersonal, and naturalistic.

Visual/spatial learners tend to think in pictures. Images created in their minds help them remember information. They like to look at maps, charts, pictures, and videos. They are good at such things as reading, writing, understanding charts and graphs, building, fixing, and designing.

Verbal/linguistic learners have the ability to use language. These learners can understand what they hear and are generally good speakers. Unlike visual learners, they think in words. Verbal/linguistic learners are good at listening, speaking, writing, teaching, remembering information, and persuading others.

Logical/mathematical learners are good at using reason, logic, and numbers. They can easily make connections between pieces of information. These learners ask many questions and like experimenting. Logical/mathematical learners are good at problem solving, classifying information, figuring out relationships between abstract concepts, doing complex mathematical calculations, and working with geometric shapes.

Bodily/kinesthetic learners express themselves with their bodies through movement.

They have good balance and coordination. By moving in the space around them, they can process and recall information. These learners are good at dancing, physical sports, acting, using body language, and expressing themselves with their bodies.

Musical/rhythmic learners have the ability to appreciate and produce music. They think in sounds, rhythms, and patterns. These learners can immediately appreciate and evaluate the music they hear. Musical/rhythmic learners are good at singing, playing instruments, writing music, and remembering tunes they hear.

Learners with interpersonal intelligence are good at relating to others. They can see things from the point of view of others and they can sense people's feelings. They are good at listening, working with others, communicating, and forming positive relationships with people.

Intrapersonal intelligence, not to be confused with interpersonal intelligence, is the ability to be aware of one's own feelings. These learners are good at self-reflecting, and they try to understand their own hopes, dreams, strengths, and weaknesses. They are good at recognizing their own abilities and feelings, reasoning with themselves, and understanding their role in relationship to other people.

Naturalistic intelligence has to do with understanding nature, that is, nurturing and relating information to one's surroundings. Naturalistic learners are sensitive to nature and have the ability to nurture and grow things.

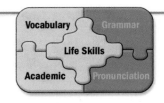

G Match each type of intelligence to the main idea associated with that type of intelligence. Write the letter of the corresponding main idea on the line after each type of intelligence.

Intelligence	Main Idea
1. visual/spatial _____	a. nurture
2. verbal/linguistic _____	b. be aware of one's feelings
3. logical/mathematical _____	c. use language
4. bodily/kinesthetic _____	d. think in pictures
5. musical/rhythmic _____	e. appreciate and produce music
6. interpersonal _____	f. express with movement
7. intrapersonal _____	g. relate well to others
8. naturalistic _____	h. use reason, logic, and numbers

H Which types of intelligence do you think are strongest in you? Write down your top three in order. (For example, if you think you are mostly musical, write that one first.)

1. _____ 2. _____ 3. _____

I How do you think the terms *learning styles* and *multiple intelligences* are related? Discuss your ideas in a small group.

J Take a class poll on learning styles and multiple intelligences. Which learning styles and types of intelligence are most common among your classmates?

Career planning

GOAL ➤ Identify a career path

A Do you have a job or a career? What is the difference between the two terms? Discuss the similarities and differences with a partner. Write your ideas in the chart below.

Job	Career

B Look up the words *job* and *career* in a dictionary. Write their definitions below.

job *n* _____

career *n* _____

C Certain careers are associated with different types of the multiple intelligences you read about in the previous lesson. Look at the list of possible careers below and guess which intelligence fits each career category. Choose the type of intelligence from the box and write it in the chart.

logical/mathematical	bodily/kinesthetic	musical/rhythmic
interpersonal	visual/spatial	intrapersonal
naturalistic	verbal/linguistic	

Intelligence	Careers
	architect, engineer, interior designer, mechanic, sculptor
	journalist, lawyer, politician, teacher, translator, writer
	accountant, computer programmer, doctor, researcher, scientist
	actor, athlete, dancer, firefighter, physical education teacher
	composer, conductor, disc jockey, musician, singer
	businessperson, counselor, politician, salesperson, social worker
	philosopher, psychologist, researcher, scientist, writer
	conservationist, farmer, gardener, scientist

D Look back at the three types of intelligence (page 5, Exercise H) you think best describe your way of processing information. Using this information, choose two careers listed on page 6 that you would be good at or interested in. Write these two careers you might like to pursue on the lines below.

_____   _____

E In a small group, discuss the two careers you chose in Exercise D. What steps do you think you would need to take to pursue one of these careers? Think about the education and training these careers require. Make note of these steps.

F In general, the more education you have, the more money you can earn. Careers that require more education usually pay more. Look at the graph below. Which two things are compared?

_____ and _____

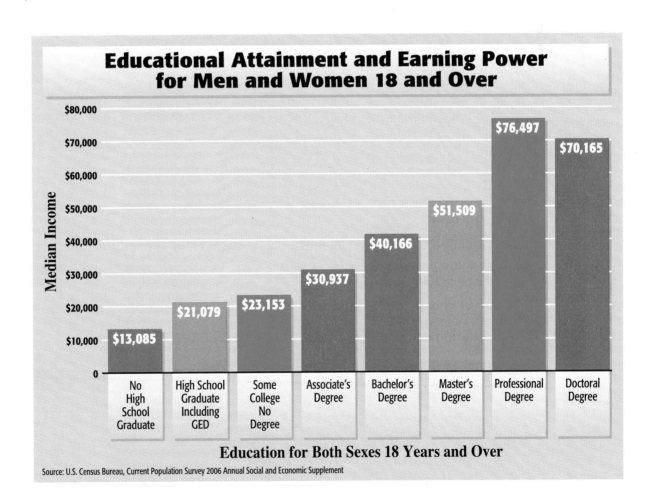

Educational Attainment and Earning Power for Men and Women 18 and Over

Median Income

- No High School Graduate: $13,085
- High School Graduate Including GED: $21,079
- Some College No Degree: $23,153
- Associate's Degree: $30,937
- Bachelor's Degree: $40,166
- Master's Degree: $51,509
- Professional Degree: $76,497
- Doctoral Degree: $70,165

Education for Both Sexes 18 Years and Over

Source: U.S. Census Bureau, Current Population Survey 2006 Annual Social and Economic Supplement

G With a partner, ask and answer the following questions. Use the information given in the graph on page 7. Replace the underlined words with different information from the graph.

> *A:* How much money can I make if I have <u>a master's degree</u>?
> *B:* About <u>$51,500</u>.

> *A:* If I want to make <u>over $70,000</u>, what education do I need?
> *B:* You need <u>a doctoral or professional degree</u>.

CD
TR 6

H Listen to the conversation between a school counselor and Sonya. Take notes on the information you hear.

1. Sonya's intelligences:

_____

2. Career she is interested in: _____

3. Education she will need: _____

4. Time it will take to get her degree and credential: _____

5. What are some other things you learned about Sonya from this conversation?

_____

_____

_____

I Think about a career path you might like to take. Fill in the information below.

1. Your intelligences: _____

2. Career you are interested in: _____

3. Education and/or training you will need: _____

4. Time it will take you to follow your career path: _____

Achieving balance

GOAL ➤ **Balance your life**

  A Sonya has many roles. Listen to her and take notes.

CD
TR 7

1. Who is Sonya? What are her roles?

_____   _____

_____   _____

_____   _____

2. Who was she? _____

_____

3. Who will she be? _____

_____

B Who are you? Write at least three statements.

I am a _____ .

_____

_____

C Who were you? Write at least two statements.

I was a _____ .

_____

_____

Review: *Be*			
Subject	***Past***	**Present**	**Future**
I	was	am	will be
you	were	are	will be
he, she, it	was	is	will be
we	were	are	will be
they	were	are	will be

D Who will you be? Write at least two statements.

I will be a _____ .

_____

E Share and discuss your information with a partner.

GOAL ➤ **Balance your life**

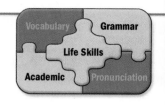

F Read what Sonya wrote and answer the questions below the paragraph with a partner.

Balance in My Life

When I was a little girl, I spent all my time playing with my two brothers. I just enjoyed doing whatever they were doing. Family was always very important to us. But as I grew older, I started working and studying more. It seemed like I was working all day, going to school every night, and studying whenever I had time. I didn't have any balance in my life. Now that I have my diploma, I don't study as much, but I still work a lot. I'm a manager at a restaurant, but I want to become an elementary school teacher. I am also a wife and a mother, and I want to spend more time with my family. So, I hope to find a job as a teacher where I can work fewer hours but still make enough money to help out. I will really enjoy being home with my family more and having more balance in my life.

1. How was Sonya's life different in the past from how it is now?
2. Is her life balanced right now? Why or why not?
3. What does she want to change in her life?
4. Do you think this change will make her happy? Why or why not?

Review: Simple Tenses				
Subject	**Past**	**Present**	**Future**	
I	spent	spend	will spend	more time with my brothers.
You	enjoyed	enjoy	will enjoy	being a mother.
He, She, It	studied	studies	will study	English every day.
We	put	put	will put	our studies first.
They	worked	work	will work	too many hours.

G Complete each statement about yourself using the tense and verb in parentheses.

EXAMPLE (*past*, want) I _wanted to be a firefighter_____.

1. (*past*, spend)   I _____.

2. (*present*, put)   I _____.

3. (*future*, live)   I _____.

4. (*present*, plan)   I _____.

5. (*future*, give)   I _____.

6. (*past*, hope)   I _____.

7. (*past*, study)   I _____.

8. (*present*, work)   I _____.

H Think about balance in your life. What are some things that are important to you? What are your interests? What activities do you do regularly? Make a list on the lines below.

_____   _____   _____

_____   _____   _____

Share your list with a partner. Is there anything you can add to your list?

I Think about how you balanced your life in the past, how you balance it now, and what you want for the future. Answer the questions below.

1. What was important to you in the past?

_____

2. What is important to you now?

_____

3. Do you spend enough time on the things that are important to you now? _____

4. What changes would you like to make for the future?

_____

J Using Sonya's paragraph in Exercise F as a writing model, write a paragraph on a piece of paper about balance in your life—past, present, and future.

K Share your paragraph with a partner and ask your partner for two suggestions about how to make your paragraph better. Share your thoughts on your partner's writing. Did your partner include interesting details? Write your partner's suggestions.

1. _____

2. _____

GOAL ➤ **Identify and prioritize goals**

A Read the flier and answer the questions below it.

1. What do you think *big picture* means?

   _____

2. What is *goal setting*?

   _____

3. Would you attend the workshop described above? Why or why not?

   _____

4. Think of three goals you set for yourself in the past. Write them down.

   a. _____

   b. _____

   c. _____

5. Did you achieve them? Write *yes* or *no* next to each goal.

B In a small group, discuss your answers to the questions in Exercise A.

CD
TR 8

Listen to the lecture on goal setting and take notes below.

Goal setting: _____

_____

_____

First thing you should do: _____

Types of goals:

1. _____   5. _____

2. _____   6. _____

3. _____   7. _____

4. _____

Tips for setting goals:

1. _____

2. _____

3. _____

4. _____

5. _____

D **Answer the following questions based on the notes you took. Circle the best answer.**

1. Which of the following is NOT true about goal setting?
   a. It will improve your self-confidence.
   b. It helps motivate you.
   c. It makes you think about your past.
   d. It helps you choose a direction for your life.

2. What are the seven types of goals?
   a. financial, physical, attitude, pleasure, education, mental, family
   b. physical, career, family, financial, attitude, personal, education
   c. education, career, technical, financial, physical, attitude, pleasure
   d. financial, physical, career, family, education, attitude, pleasure

3. Why is it important to prioritize your goals in a list?
   a. It will be easy to know when you have achieved a goal.
   b. It will help you focus your attention on the most important goals.
   c. It gives them life.
   d. It will improve your self-confidence.

GOAL ➤ **Identify and prioritize goals**

E Sonya attended the goal-setting workshop and created a list of goals that she now keeps on her refrigerator.

I can do it!

➔ *The Big Picture:* ◄

*I plan to be successful in my personal and professional life.
I will be a highly educated elementary school teacher.*

SHORT-TERM GOALS
- *spend more time with my children*
- *exercise to reduce stress*
- *enroll in community college*

LONG-TERM GOALS
- *get my Bachelor's degree and teaching credentials*
- *become an elementary school teacher*
- *get a master's degree*
- *learn how to swim*

F Sonya's goals are prioritized (listed in order of importance). Do you think she put her goals in the right order? Discuss your ideas with a partner.

G The Big Picture: Think about where you would like to be ten years from now. Based on your thoughts, what are your long-term goals? Use the items below to help you clarify what your goals should be.

1. Write one goal for each category.

   Education: _____

   Career: _____

   Family: _____

   Financial: _____

   Physical: _____

   Attitude: _____

   Pleasure: _____

2. Number your three most important goals above in order of priority.

3. Based on these three long-term goals, what are some short-term goals you can set in order to help you reach the long-term ones?

   Short-term goals: _____

   _____

4. Prioritize your short-term goals. Write them in order. _____

   _____

LESSON 5

Motivation

GOAL ➤ Motivate yourself

Vocabulary | Grammar
Life Skills
Academic | Pronunciation

A Are you motivated to achieve your goals? Do you need someone to motivate you? Can you motivate yourself?

Define *motivation* (your own definition or one from a dictionary): _____

_____

B How can you motivate yourself to reach your goals? Work with a small group and make a list.

Ways We Can Motivate Ourselves

_____   _____

_____   _____

_____   _____

_____   _____

  C Listen to Mrs. Morgan's students talk about motivating themselves. Take notes about what each person says.

CD
TR 9

 Liam: _____    Sonya: _____

_____   _____

 Haru: _____    Rani: _____

_____   _____

 Kimla: _____    Mario: _____

_____   _____

D What idea for getting motivated does each person have? Share what you recall with a partner.

Vocabulary | Grammar
Life Skills
Academic | Pronunciation

E Below is a list of things you can do to motivate yourself toward pursuing a goal. Which of the following steps do you already do? Which of the following steps would you like to do? Put checks in the correct column.

I already do this.	I would like to do this.	Steps to motivate yourself toward pursuing a goal
_____	_____	1. Write down your goals and put them in a place you will see them every day.
_____	_____	2. Tell family and friends about your goals so they can support you.
_____	_____	3. Tell yourself that you can do it.
_____	_____	4. Keep a positive attitude.
_____	_____	5. Be enthusiastic about your goals.
_____	_____	6. When you slow down or don't have the energy to do anything, take small steps and continue moving forward. Don't stop.
_____	_____	7. Evaluate your progress. Make a chart or do something to monitor progress.
_____	_____	8. Don't be too fixed on one approach. Be flexible and make changes when needed.
_____	_____	9. Read inspiring books.
_____	_____	10. Take some time to refresh yourself.
_____	_____	11. Exercise will help your attitude. "The better your health, the more positive your outlook."
_____	_____	12. After you are motivated, motivate others.

F One of the best ways to motivate yourself is to keep a positive attitude and remind yourself of your goals every day. Read the statements below and write the name of the person who said each statement. (Mrs. Morgan, Haru, Liam, Rani, Kimla, Sonya)

1. I will already have become a teacher by the time my kids are in school. _____

2. When I turn 35, I will have been a graphic designer for five years. _____

3. By the time my grandkids go to college, I will have gone on three photography expeditions. _____

4. I will have registered for college by the time I finish my last English class. _____

5. I will have been a teacher of English for 20 years when I retire. _____

6. By the time I finish my nursing program, I will have found a job at a local hospital. _____

G Study the chart with your teacher.

Future Perfect Tense				
Subject	*will have*	Past participle		Future event—Time expression
I	will have	become	a teacher	by the time my kids are in school.
He	will have	been	a graphic designer (for five years)	when he turns 35.
They	will have	found	a job	by 2015.

We use the future perfect to talk about an activity that will be completed before another time or event in the future. ──┤present ──✗── future to be completed (perfect) ──✗── future event with time expression

Note: The order of events is not important. If the future event with the time expression comes first, use a comma.

Example: *By the time my kids are in school, I will have become a teacher.*

H Mrs. Morgan's other students wrote goal statements as well. Complete each statement with the correct form of the future perfect of the verb in parentheses.

1. By the time I graduate from high school, I (do) _____ 500 hours of community service.

2. I (buy) _____ a new house when I retire.

3. When I turn 60, I (travel) _____ to over 20 countries.

4. We (put) _____ three kids through college by 2020.

5. I (become) _____ a successful business owner by the time I turn 40.

6. By the time I finish getting my degree, I (apply) _____ to three different graduate programs.

I Write three goal statements for yourself on a separate piece of paper.

J Now that you have written down your goals, what are you going to do to keep yourself motivated? Write down three ideas on a separate piece of paper. Share your goals and motivation with a partner.

Review

A Indicate the learning style next to each activity. Write *V* for *Visual*, *A* for *Auditory*, and *T/K* for *Tactile/Kinesthetic* on the line. (Lesson 1)

1. analyzing a graph _____

2. listening to a discussion _____

3. listening to a lecture _____

4. participating in a dance _____

5. reading a journal article _____

6. touching objects _____

7. watching an online newscast _____

B Complete each statement with a phrase from the box. (Lesson 1)

appreciates music	relates well to surroundings
expresses oneself with movement	thinks in pictures
is aware of one's own feelings	uses language
relates well to others	uses reason, logic, and numbers

1. A naturalistic person _____.

2. Someone with interpersonal intelligence _____.

3. A person who is kinesthetic _____.

4. A logical/mathematical person _____.

5. A person with visual intelligence _____.

6. Someone with intrapersonal intelligence _____.

7. A musical/rhythmic person _____.

8. A verbal/linguistic person _____.

C Interview a classmate about how the information below relates to him or her. Write his or her answers on the lines. (Lessons 2–3)

1. Types of intelligence: _____

2. Career interests: _____

3. What is important to you now? _____

4. What changes would you like to make for your future? _____

D   Write a paragraph about your partner on a separate piece of paper. (Lesson 3)

E   Remember what you learned about goal setting. Without looking back in the unit, write four tips for setting goals. (Lesson 4)

1. _____

2. _____

3. _____

4. _____

F   Walk around the classroom and ask your classmates for suggestions on how to motivate yourself. Write five ideas below. (Lesson 5)

1. _____

2. _____

3. _____

4. _____

5. _____

G   Choose a verb from the box below and complete each goal statement with the correct form of the future perfect. (Lesson 5)

buy and sell	raise	program
apply	compete	

1. By the time I graduate from technical school, I _____ over twenty computers.

2. She _____ at least ten properties when she retires.

3. When he turns 65, he _____ two amazing children.

4. They _____ in their first triathlon by the year 2012.

5. By the time I get my Master's Degree, I _____ for forty jobs at companies all over the country.

VOCABULARY REVIEW

H Use these words to help you complete all the exercises on this page. Some words may be used more than once.

achieve	evaluate	positive outlook
balance	inspire	prioritize
be flexible	long-term	pursue
earning power	monitor	short-term
educational attainment	motivate	support

I Complete each sentence with the best verb. Note that some sentences can have more than one answer. Then, work with a partner and use the five questions for a discussion.

1. If you _____ your goals, you can focus on the most important ones first.

2. Have you ever created a chart to _____ your progress?

3. What career do you think you might _____?

4. How do you _____ yourself?

5. What goals have you _____ in the past?

6. Have you found family and friends to _____ you?

J Write sentences about goal setting with the following terms.

1. balance: _____

2. be flexible: _____

3. positive outlook: _____

4. achieve: _____

K Complete each phrase below. Use a word from the box above and your own words.

1. To improve your earning power, you should _____

_____

2. If you want to achieve your goals, you must _____

_____

3. In order to best reach your long-term goals, you have to _____

_____.

Research Project

A One of the fastest ways to research something is to search the Internet. For example, you might want to know how much money you can make at a certain career. What are some key words you could use to search for this information?

_____

B If you have access to the Internet, conduct an online search to find out the following information for the career path that you chose in Lesson 2, Exercise I.

Career title: _____

Training needed: _____

Education needed: _____

Possible earnings: _____

C The U.S. Department of Labor, Bureau of Labor Statistics (http://www.bls.gov/home.htm) publishes the *Occupational Outlook Handbook* every two years. This handbook gives information about hundreds of different types of jobs. In this handbook, you will find the following types of information: the training and education needed, earnings, expected job prospects, what workers do on the job, and working conditions.

The following topics are from the *Occupational Outlook Handbook.* Which one do you think would have information about your career? Underline it.

Management, Business, and Financial
   Occupations
Engineers, Life and Physical Scientists,
   and Related Occupations
Arts, Design, Entertainment, Sports,
   and Media Occupations
Education and Community and Social
   Service Occupations
Computer and Mathematical Occupations
Legal and Social Science Occupations
Health Diagnosing and Treating Practitioners
Health Technologists, Technicians, and
   Healthcare Support Occupations

Service Occupations: Cleaning, Food,
   and Personal
Protective Service Occupations
Sales Occupations
Office and Administrative Support
   Occupations
Farming, Fishing, Forestry, and
   Transportation Occupations
Construction Trades and Related
   Occupations
Installation, Maintenance, and Repair
   Occupations
Production Occupations

D Find the *Occupational Outlook Handbook* online at http://www.bls.gov/oco/. Search for the information about your chosen career. Print out the information to research.

Team Project

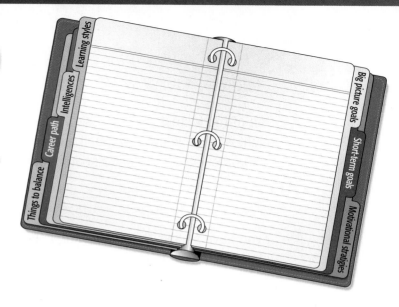

Create a personal profile.

With a team, decide on one of these project options:
a. Create a profile for yourself.
   (one profile per group member)
b. Create a profile for an imaginary person.
   (one profile per group)

1. Form a team with four or five students. Choose a position for each member of your team.

POSITION	JOB DESCRIPTION	STUDENT NAME
Student 1: **Project Leader**	See that everyone speaks English. See that everyone participates.	
Student 2: **Secretary**	Take notes on team's ideas. Write a list of items to include in profile.	
Student 3: **Designer**	Design profile.	
Student 4: **Spokesperson**	Report information to the class if team creates one profile for an imaginary person. Otherwise, prepare team members for individual presentations.	
Student 5: **Assistant**	Help the secretary and designer with their work.	

2. Discuss and decide on profile information: learning style, intelligence(s), career path, things to balance in life, short- and long-term goals, and a list of motivational strategies.*

3. Decide on the design. Organize the layout of the profile.

4. Present profile to the class.

* *Options:* If your team is creating individual profiles, work together to decide what general information will go in each person's profile as well as how to organize the profiles. Team members then complete profiles on their own.

Personal Finance

GOALS

➤ Organize your finances
➤ Reduce debt and save money
➤ Identify investment strategies

➤ Maintain good credit
➤ Protect yourself against identity theft

Vocabulary Builder

A Kimla sat down and made a list of her financial goals. Read what she wrote.

My Financial Goals

1. I need to stop *impulse buying* and pay off my credit cards.
2. I want to stop *living paycheck to paycheck* and save enough money for a down payment on a house.
3. I want to increase my *purchasing power* by putting $200 a month into an emergency savings account.
4. I want us to start *living within our means*, so I can start giving $100 a month to charity.
5. I want to *save* $75 a month, so I can attend college next year.

B What does each of the italicized expressions mean? Discuss them with your classmates.

C Some English phrases, such as *living paycheck to paycheck* or *living within your means*, have a special meaning. Often, if you try to understand the meaning of the individual words, you can understand the phrase. Talk to your classmates or use a dictionary to discover the meaning of the following expressions.

1. budget cut
2. buy in bulk
3. capital gains
4. commit fraud
5. counterfeit checks
6. current income
7. delinquent accounts
8. false pretenses
9. unauthorized transactions

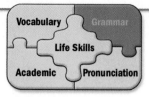

D Look at the following sentences. Try to figure out the meaning of the underlined words by reading them in context.

1. The company declared <u>bankruptcy</u> when it ran out of money.

   Bankruptcy means _____.

2. I took out a loan at the bank and used my house as <u>collateral</u>.

   Collateral means _____.

3. The thought of starting a business was <u>daunting</u>, but he decided to do it anyway.

   Daunting means _____.

4. <u>Inflation</u> was so great that bread cost twice as much in June as it did in May.

   Inflation means _____.

5. His <u>investment</u> in the stock market has made him a millionaire.

   Investment means _____.

6. The company has no <u>liquid</u> assets; therefore, it can't pay its bills.

   Liquid means _____.

7. She paid the <u>penalty</u> of a large fine for cheating on her income tax returns.

   Penalty means _____.

8. He <u>periodically</u> reviews his budget and makes changes when necessary.

   Periodically means _____.

9. Putting money in the stock market might be <u>risky</u> because you could lose your money.

   Risky means _____.

E Look back at Kimla's financial goals in Exercise A on page 23. Using some of the new vocabulary words and phrases you have learned in this lesson, write four of your own financial goals.

1. _____

2. _____

3. _____

4. _____

Getting organized

GOAL ➤ **Organize your finances**

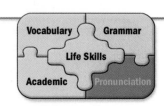

A Look back at the goals you wrote in Exercise E on page 24. Rewrite the goals below, giving each one a time frame.

EXAMPLE: <u>By the end of next year, I will have paid off my credit cards.</u>

1. _____
2. _____
3. _____
4. _____

B Do you know how much money you spend a week? A month? A year? Many people are not certain of the exact amount it costs them to live. Often, people don't include the expenses that come up occasionally in their personal budgets.

Think about how you spend your money. Answer the following questions.

1. Did you go on a vacation last year? _____ How much did it cost? _____

2. Do you know how much you spend during the holidays every year? _____

3. How often do you get your hair cut? _____ How much does it cost? _____

4. How often do you pay car insurance premiums? _____ How much is each

premium? _____

C Listen to a financial planner talking about how to organize personal finances. Write down the most important points the planner makes.

CD
TR 10

1. _____
_____
2. _____
_____
3. _____
_____
4. _____
5. _____

D Compare your notes with a partner. Add any important points you missed.

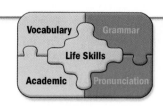

LESSON 1   GOAL ➤ Organize your finances

E   After meeting with a financial planner, Kimla and her husband sat down with all of their bank statements, credit card statements, ATM records, and receipts. Look at the worksheet below that they created. What do they still need to calculate?

MONEY OUT		
	Annual	**Monthly**
Mortgage/Rent	_____	$1,700
Home maintenance fees		$200
Renters' insurance	$500	_____
Gas & Electric	_____	$150
Water		$20
Telephone/Cell phone	_____	$130
Food/Restaurants	_____	$300
Medical/Dental		$85
Auto expenses	_____	$160
Tolls/Fares/Parking	_____	$30
Clothes/Shoes	$850	_____
Dry cleaning	_____	$15
Hair/Manicure/Facial		$50
Kids' school	$500	_____
Training/Education	$300	_____
Income taxes	$655	_____
Computer	_____	$50
Credit cards/Loans	_____	$650
Postage	_____	$3
Subscriptions	$24	_____
Entertainment	_____	$50
Cable/Satellite	_____	$65
Vacations	$2,000	_____
Hobbies	$175	_____
Gifts	$550	_____
TOTAL	_____	_____

Calculations

To calculate annual expenses, multiple monthly expense by 12:

$$250 \times 12 = 3000 \qquad 15 \times 12 = 180 \qquad 55 \times 12 \qquad 1300 \times 12$$

To calculate monthly expenses, divide annual expense by 12:

$$3000 \div 12 = 250 \qquad 180 \div 12 = 15$$
$$\underline{\hspace{1cm}} \div 12 = 55 \qquad \underline{\hspace{1cm}} \div 12 = 1300$$

F   Calculate Kimla and her husband's annual and monthly totals.

G   Together, Kimla and her husband make about $53,000 a year before deductions. How much do they have left over? _____ How much is this per month? _____ Do you think Kimla's family lives within their means? Why? or Why not? _____
_____

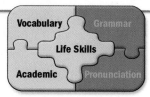

H In Kimla and her husband's Money Out Worksheet on the previous page, some expenses are *fixed* (stay the same every month) and others are *variable* (can change from month to month). With a partner, make a list of Kimla and her husband's fixed expenses and a list of their variable expenses.

Fixed	Variable

I Look back at Kimla's financial goals on page 23. How much money does she want to start saving per month for college? _____ For charity? _____ For emergencies? _____ Does she have enough money in her budget for these items? _____ If not, what expenses do you think Kimla and her husband can cut back on? Look at the list of variable expenses you made in Exercise H and discuss your ideas with a group.

J Create a Money Out worksheet like the one on page 26, listing all the monthly and annual expenses you have. Next to each expense, write *f* for a fixed expense or *v* for a variable expense. Look at the chart below to get you started.

	Annual	Monthly
Mortgage (f)		
Home maintenance fees (v)		
Homeowner's insurance (f)		
Gas & Electric (v)		
Water (v)		

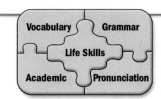

LESSON 2 Managing money

GOAL ➤ **Reduce debt and save money**

A Read the ad.

WE CAN HELP

Do you live within your means or do you live paycheck to paycheck?

Do you owe money to a bank or another person?

Are you up to your ears in debt?

The first thing we will help you do is make a budget. It is important to plan out your monthly expenses so you know where your money is going each month. Our advisors will help you get on track so you can make some cuts to your monthly budget. These cuts will allow you to pay off your debt faster. We'll show you how to get rid of bad debt by paying off your higher interest and long-term debts first. We'll get your credit reports for you and analyze them to see if we can help boost your credit rating. We'll also teach you some helpful tips; here's one: *Credit card interest is calculated daily, so if you make your payment earlier than the due date, you'll actually save interest*! If there are some debts that you just can't pay, we'll contact the creditors and arrange settlements for you.

How can you afford not to let us help you?   **Don't hesitate.**   Call us today! (800) 555-0125

B Answer the questions about the ad with a partner.

1. Who do you think wrote this ad? _____

2. What is the purpose of this ad? (Why was it written?) _____

_____

3. Would you call the number listed at the bottom of the ad? Why or why not?

_____

4. The ad mentions how they would help get you out of debt. List four of their suggestions.

    a. _____

    b. _____

    c. _____

    d. _____

C   The ad on page 28 mentions making cuts to your budget. Read the Web page below with tips on how to save money.

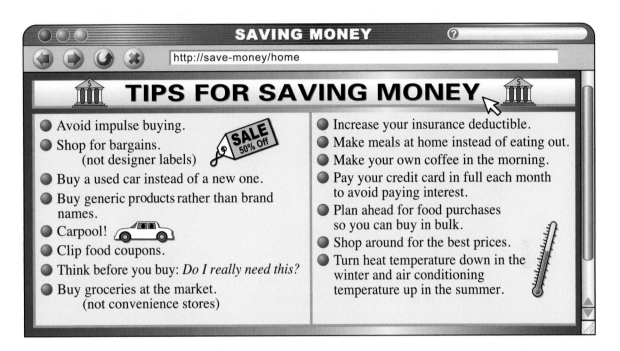

SAVING MONEY   ?

http://save-money/home

TIPS FOR SAVING MONEY

- Avoid impulse buying.
- Shop for bargains. (not designer labels)
- Buy a used car instead of a new one.
- Buy generic products rather than brand names.
- Carpool!
- Clip food coupons.
- Think before you buy: *Do I really need this?*
- Buy groceries at the market. (not convenience stores)

- Increase your insurance deductible.
- Make meals at home instead of eating out.
- Make your own coffee in the morning.
- Pay your credit card in full each month to avoid paying interest.
- Plan ahead for food purchases so you can buy in bulk.
- Shop around for the best prices.
- Turn heat temperature down in the winter and air conditioning temperature up in the summer.

 D   Listen to Kimla and her husband, Derek, talk about saving money. Write *T (true)* or *F (false)* on the line before each statement.

CD
TR 11

_____ 1. Kimla buys designer clothes.

_____ 2. Derek had been buying his coffee at a coffee shop.

_____ 3. Kimla had been paying high interest on credit cards.

_____ 4. Derek had been looking at new cars.

_____ 5. Kimla turns off the air conditioner before she goes to bed.

_____ 6. Derek called the insurance to increase their deductible.

_____ 7. Kimla has never bought generic products.

_____ 8. Derek clips coupons.

 E   Do you already follow some of the tips in the ad in Exercise C? Which ones? Put a check (✔) next to the ones you are familiar with. Which ones would you like to follow in the future? Underline these tips.

GOAL ➤ **Reduce debt and save money**

F Study the chart with your teacher.

Past Perfect Continuous Tense					
First event in past					**Second event in past**
Subject	***had***	***been***	**Verb + *-ing***		
Kimla	had	been	buying	designer clothes	before she started bargain shopping.
He	had	been	buying	coffee at a coffee shop	before he began making it at home.
They	had	been	paying	a lower deductible	before they called the insurance company.

- We use the past perfect continuous to talk about an activity that was happening for a while before another event happened in the past. For the most recent event, we use the simple past tense.

- Remember to use a comma if you put the second event as the first part of the sentence. Example: Before she started bargain shopping, Kimla had been buying designer clothes.

G Think about your past behavior and how you have changed it to reduce debt and save money. Write four statements.

EXAMPLE: <u>I had been eating out for lunch every day before I started making</u>

<u>my lunch at home.</u>

1. _____

2. _____

3. _____

4. _____

H Come up with three ways in which you are going to change your behavior to reduce debt and save money.

EXAMPLE: <u>Tomorrow, I will start making my lunch at home.</u>

1. _____

2. _____

3. _____

Investing wisely

GOAL ➤ **Identify investment strategies**

A In a small group, look at the following list of vocabulary words and phrases. Which words do you know? How can you find out the meaning of the ones you don't know? Discuss ways with your group and then, with your group, use those ways to find the meanings.

1. capital gains: _____

2. convert: _____

3. inflation: _____

4. liquid: _____

5. net appreciation: _____

6. penalty: _____

7. purchasing power: _____

8. risky: _____

9. value: _____

10. vehicle: _____

B Words often have more than one meaning. It is important to know what you are listening to or reading so you can find the correct part of speech and definition for the new vocabulary word. Look at the meaning you wrote for *vehicle*. Compare your definition with this definition.

vehicle: a way in which something is accomplished

C Based on the words you defined above, what do you think the article below is about? Discuss your ideas with your classmates.

D Read the article about investing money.

THE CHICKEN OR THE MARKET?

By Andrew Rothemer

I once knew a family who kept their life savings in a chicken in the freezer. My grandmother kept a stash of cash under her mattress. I think my wife has a secret hiding place in the drawer next to the bed. Where do you keep your life savings?

Investing can be risky, so many people prefer to find a safe place to put their money at home. But keeping your money in a drawer, under a mattress, or even in a chicken will eventually decrease your purchasing power. Due to inflation, money is worth less and less each year, so by not investing your money, you are actually losing money. In order to prevent inflation from destroying the value of your money, you need to invest. Let's take a look at some basic kinds of investments.

(continued)

An investment can make you money in three basic ways. First, an investment can earn *current income*. Current income is money that you receive periodically, for example, every month or every six months. An example of an investment that provides current income is a certificate of deposit (CD) because interest is paid to your account periodically. A second way that an investment can make money is through *capital growth*. This is when the amount of money you have invested grows in value over time. When you sell the investment, you get your money back plus any increase in value. Examples of capital growth investments are stocks and other assets that you own, such as your home. Finally, a third way that an investment can earn income is through a combination of current income and capital growth. Examples include rental property and stocks that pay dividends, that is, extra or bonus amounts of money.

So, which type of investment is best for you? That will depend on your age and income. Younger investors who are working and earning a steady income may not need to earn current income from their investments. They may be more interested in capital growth. On the other hand, older investors who are retired and living on limited social security and pension funds are more likely to be interested in earning current income from their investments. There are many different ways to invest your money, but let's look at five of the most widely used investment vehicles.

Probably the most popular investment vehicle is the savings account, which offers low minimum deposits, liquidity (the ability to withdraw and deposit whenever you want), and insurance protection. Because of these features, savings accounts pay relatively low interest rates. Another investment vehicle that is somewhat similar to a savings account in that it offers low interest rates and insurance protection is a certificate of deposit (CD). A CD requires that you put money in and leave it for a certain amount of time—three months, six months, a year, etc. Usually, the longer the amount of time you keep it in, the higher the interest. CDs are not perfectly liquid because early withdrawal of funds from a CD often results in a penalty. Another type of investment is a mutual fund where a number of investors put their money together to buy specific investments. Some mutual funds invest in stocks, some in bonds, and some in real estate. The mutual fund investor owns shares of the fund, not the actual stocks, bonds, or property purchased by the fund. Most likely, when a person thinks of investing, he or she probably thinks of the stock market. Ownership of a stock represents ownership of a *claim* on the net earnings of a company. Therefore, stock earnings depend on how well the company is doing. Stocks can be quickly converted to cash by selling them on the stock market, but because the price of stocks changes daily, there is no guarantee that you will get back the money that you paid for the stock. And finally, property or real estate is a popular investment because it can produce returns in two ways: current income and net appreciation (capital gains). You can receive current income if the property is used, such as in situations where tenants are renting it or if crops are grown on the land. Net appreciation occurs if the property increases in value during the time that you own it. A major disadvantage of real estate and rental property is that they are not very liquid; it takes time and resources to turn them into cash. It may take many months to sell a piece of property.

So, which investment will be best for you? Only you can decide. Think carefully about your financial situation, how much money you can or want to invest, and how soon you will need access to the money. I can guarantee that whatever investment vehicle you choose, you will benefit more than if you keep your cash in a chicken!

 E **Discuss the following questions with a partner.**

1. Do you invest your money? If so, how do you invest it?
2. What investment vehicles would you like to try?
3. Would you say you are conservative with your money? Why or why not?

F Use the ideas you have learned about investment strategies in this lesson to complete the sentences below. Each sentence may have more than one answer.

1. If you don't invest your money, you will lose _____ over time.

2. The _____ of stocks is based on the earnings of the company.

3. Savings accounts and mutual funds are not very _____.

4. My favorite investment _____ is _____ (your own idea).

5. It is not easy to _____ real estate into cash.

6. Savings accounts are very _____. You can get the cash whenever you need it.

G An outline is a way to organize the main ideas of something you have listened to or read. You can write notes or complete sentences in an outline, but do not directly copy the author's words. Based on the reading in Exercise D, complete the outline below.

I. Investing is risky.
   A. _____
   B. _____
   C. _____

II. Investments make you money.
   A. Current income
   B. _____
   C. _____

III. Investment type will depend on age and income.
   A. _____
   B. _____

IV. Popular investment types
   A. _____
   B. _____
   C. Stocks
   D. _____
   E. _____

H A summary is a brief statement of main ideas. On a separate piece of paper, write a one-paragraph summary of the investing article using the notes from your outline.

Credit

GOAL ➤ Maintain good credit

(A) In a small group, discuss the following questions.

1. What is credit?

2. What makes credit good or bad?

3. How can you find out if you have good or bad credit?

4. If you have bad credit, how can you improve it?

(B) Read the article below. As you read it, underline the main ideas.

THE FOUR KEYS TO GREAT CREDIT

By Liz Pulliam Weston

Your credit history can make or break you when trying to convince lenders you're a good risk. Here's how to build the best record you can—before you need it.

Getting credit when you don't have any—or when you're recovering from a credit disaster such as bankruptcy—can be daunting. Without a good credit history, it's hard to get new credit. But without credit, it's tough to build a good credit history. Tough, but far from impossible. Every day, people take steps that establish and improve their image in the eyes of lenders. So can you. Here's what you need to do:

✔ **Open checking and savings accounts.**

Having bank accounts establishes you as part of the financial mainstream. Lenders want to know you have a checking account available to pay bills, and a savings account indicates you're putting aside something for the future.

Opening bank accounts is something you can do even if you're too young to establish credit in your own name. Until you're 18, you can't legally be held to a contract, so any credit you get will have to be through an adult—either someone who cosigns a loan for you, adds

you to their credit cards, or opens a joint account with you. Having bank accounts, though, gets you started on the right path and gives you practice in managing your money.

✔ **Get your credit report—if you have one.**

Next, you need to find out how lenders view you. Most lenders base their decisions on credit reports, which are compiled by for-profit companies known as credit bureaus. You are entitled to a free credit report from each of the three major bureaus each year.

Typically, a credit report includes identifying information about you, such as your name, address, social security number, and birth date. The report may also list any credit accounts or loans opened in your name, along with your payment history, account limits, and unpaid balances.

If you're young or newly arrived in the United States, you may not have a report or it may have little information. If you've had credit problems, your report will list them.

(continued)

✔ **Fix any errors or omissions.**

Some credit reports include errors—accounts that don't belong to you or that include out-of-date or misleading information. You should read through each of your three reports and note anything that's incorrect.

Negative information, such as late payments, delinquencies, liens, and judgments against you, should be dropped after seven years. Bankruptcies can stay on your report for up to ten years.

Once you have a list of problems, ask the bureaus to investigate errors listed on their reports. You can use the form that comes with your report if you receive it by mail, or you can use the Web link if you accessed your report on the Internet.

✔ **Add positive information to your report.**

The more information you can provide about yourself, the more comfortable lenders may feel extending credit to you. In addition, certain information—such as having the same job or address for a few years—can make you appear more stable in lenders' eyes.

While this information isn't used in creating your credit score, it is often used by lenders when they make lending decisions. You may also find that your report doesn't include credit accounts or other information that it should. Here's a list of items to consider:

• Are your employer and your job title listed? If you've had the job less than two years, your previous employer and job title should be listed as well.
• Is your address listed and correct? If you've been at your current address less than two years, is your previous address listed as well?
• Is your social security number listed and correct? This is the way most lenders will identify you.
• Is your telephone number listed and correct? Many lenders may not extend credit if they can't call you to verify information.

• Does your report include all the accounts you've paid on time? Some lenders don't report regularly to credit bureaus, and some report to only one or two, rather than all three. You can ask the creditor to report the account to a bureau that doesn't list it. If the creditor refuses or doesn't respond, you can send a letter to the bureau with a copy of your latest statement and canceled checks to prove you're paying on time.

✔ **Establish credit.**

There are three common routes for establishing new credit:

1. Apply for department store and gasoline cards. These are usually easier to get than major bank credit cards.
2. Consider taking out a small personal loan from your local bank or credit union and paying the money back over time. The bank may require you to put up some collateral—such as the same amount you're borrowing, deposited into a savings account. But the loan, if reported to the credit bureaus, can still help build your credit history. Make sure that it will be reported before you borrow the money.
3. Apply for a secured credit card. These work something like the loan described above: You deposit a certain amount at a bank, and in return you're given a Visa or MasterCard with a credit limit roughly equal to the amount you deposited. You can find a list of secured cards at www.bankrate.com. Avoid any card that charges a big upfront fee for processing your application or a high annual fee.

✔ **Once you've got credit, use it right.**

Charge small amounts on each card—but never more than you can pay off each month. You need to use credit regularly to establish your credit history, but there's usually no advantage to paying interest on those charges.

(continued)

Vocabulary · Grammar · Life Skills · Academic · Pronunciation

Once you've been approved for one card or loan, don't rush out and apply for several more. Applying for too much credit will hurt, rather than help, your score. Most people need only one or two bank cards, a gasoline card, and a department store card—acquired over a year or more—to start a solid credit history.

Pay your bills on time, all the time. This includes household bills, such as utilities and telephone, as well as your credit card bills and loans. Late payments on any of these accounts can wind up in your credit report and can really hurt your credit score—the three-digit number widely used by lenders to evaluate your creditworthiness.

Don't max out your credit cards. In fact, don't even come close. Try to avoid using more than 30% or so of the credit you have available to you—even less, if you can. Your credit score measures the difference between the credit available to you and what you're actually using. The smaller that gap, the more it hurts your score. Lenders will worry that you're becoming overextended and won't be able to pay your bills if you charge too much.

Liz Pulliam Weston is a personal finance columnist for MSN Money (http://money.msn.com), where this article first appeared. Used by permission. Her column appears every Monday and Thursday, exclusively on MSN Money. She also answers reader questions in the Your Money message board.

C Imagine you are a financial advisor. Give your partner advice based on the following questions.

1. What can I do to establish good credit?

2. What should I look for in my credit report?

3. How can I add positive information to my credit report?

D Go back through the article and underline any words or phrases you do not understand. Work with a partner and a dictionary to discover their meanings. Write them in your notebook.

E On a separate piece of paper, make an outline of Ms. Weston's article. Then, write a summary.

F Having read the article, what are four things you need to do to help establish or maintain your credit?

1. _____

2. _____

3. _____

4. _____

LESSON 5 Identity theft

GOAL ➤ **Protect yourself against identity theft**

CD
TR 12

A Listen to each of the following people talk about their financial problems. What happened? Take notes on the lines below each photo.

1. _____

2. _____

3. _____

B Have you ever had any problems with your credit similar to the ones in Exercise A? If so, what did you do about it? Tell your classmates about it.

C In a small group, discuss the following questions.

1. What is identity theft?

2. What do you think the following terms mean: *dumpster diving, skimming, phishing,* and *pretexting*?

3. What are some things a person who steals your identify might do? Come up with some ideas in addition to the three from Exercise A.

4. What can you do if someone steals your identity?

  D

CD
TR 13

LESSON 5 GOAL ► Protect yourself against identity theft

Listen to an interview with a member of the Federal Trade Comission (FTC). In each question below, one answer is NOT correct. Choose the incorrect answer.

1. What is identity theft?
   a. when someone uses your credit card number without permission to buy things
   b. when someone steals your name and social security number to commit crimes
   c. when someone commits fraud using your personal information
   d. when someone asks you for your personal information

2. What are some ways thieves steal your identity?
   a. dumpster diving
   b. changing your name
   c. stealing
   d. skimming

3. An example of bank fraud is . . .
   a. when someone takes out a loan in your name.
   b. when someone gets a driver's license in your name.
   c. when someone opens an account in your name.
   d. when someone creates counterfeit checks using your account number.

4. How can you find out if your identity has been stolen?
   a. cancel credit card accounts
   b. monitor bank accounts
   c. check credit reports
   d. check my bank statements

5. What should you do if your identity has been stolen?
   a. notify creditors
   b. try to find the thief
   c. file a police report
   d. check credit reports

6. How can you help fight identity theft?
   a. donate money to the Federal Trade Commission
   b. be aware of how information is stolen
   c. monitor personal information
   d. educate friends and family about identity theft

E   Using the information provided from the questions in Exercise D, work with a group to write a summary about identify theft.

_____

_____

_____

_____

_____

_____

_____

_____

_____

_____

_____

_____

F   In your group, use your summary to prepare a presentation that will educate your classmates about identity theft. Answer the questions below.

1. What information will you present to the class? _____

_____

2. How will you present your information? (orally only, orally and visually, etc.)

_____

3. Who will present which part of the presentation? (Everyone in your group must participate.)

_____

_____

Review

A Roger and Rupert are brothers who live together. Complete their Money Out Worksheet below by filling in the missing numbers. (Lesson 1)

MONEY OUT		
	Annual	**Monthly**
Rent	_____	$2,200
Home maintenance fees	_____	$150
Renters' insurance	$600	_____
Gas & Electric	_____	$220
Water	_____	$40
Telephone/Cell phone	_____	$120
Food/Restaurants	_____	$275
Medical/Dental	_____	$140
Auto expenses	_____	$890
Clothes/Shoes	$1,125	_____
Hair/Manicure/Facial	_____	$125
Training/Education	$700	_____
Income taxes	$824	_____
Computer	_____	$75
Credit cards/Loans	_____	$975
Entertainment	_____	$250
Cable/Satellite TV	_____	$65
Vacations	$500	_____
Gifts	$795	_____
TOTAL		

Together, Roger and Rupert make about $72,000 a year.

1. How much do they have left over per year? _____

2. How much do they have left over per month? _____

3. Do you think Roger and Rupert live within their means? _____

4. What suggestions would you make for curbing their spending?

a. _____

b. _____

c. _____

d. _____

B Write four tips for saving money. (Lesson 2)

1. _____ 3. _____

2. _____ 4. _____

C Complete each statement with the past perfect continuous or the simple past. (Lesson 2)

EXAMPLE: Erika _____had been buying_____ lunch every day before she

_____started_____ making it at home.

1. Justin _____ (charge) his credit cards to their maximum limits

before he _____ (cut) them up.

2. Before the Ingrams _____ (buy) a new car, they

_____ (lease) a used one.

3. We _____ (live) beyond our means before we

_____ (organize) our finances.

4. Before she _____ (research) insurance rates, she

_____ (spend) too much on auto insurance.

(D) Write four things you have learned about investing on a piece of paper. Share your ideas with a partner. Add two ideas that your partner came up with. (Lesson 3)

(E) Answer the following questions by yourself or with a partner. (Lesson 4)

1. What is credit? _____

2. What can you do to establish good credit? _____

3. What makes credit good or bad? _____

4. How can you find out if you have good or bad credit? _____

5. If you have bad credit, how can you improve it? _____

6. What should you look for in your credit report? _____

7. How can you add positive information to your credit report? _____

(F) Read each scenario. Write what you think happened and what the person should do to fix the problem. (Lesson 5)

1. Marika tried to withdraw money from her ATM account, which had over $1,000 in it the last time she checked it, but the bank said she had insufficient funds.

What happened? _____

Solution: _____

2. Marco noticed some unfamiliar charges on his credit card statement.

What happened? _____

Solution: _____

3. The IRS contacted Frankie and said he never paid income tax on a second job, which he didn't have.

What happened? _____

Solution: _____

VOCABULARY REVIEW

G A *synonym* is a word that has the same meaning as another word. Look at each of the words below and choose a word from the box that is its synonym.

1. income _____

2. fake _____

3. late _____

4. scam _____

5. cost _____

6. good deal _____

7. money due _____

8. liability _____

9. change _____

10. value _____

bargain	delinquent	fraud
convert	earnings	risk
counterfeit	expense	worth
debt		

H Look back in the unit and find three new terms you learned (different from the words in the box above). Write a sentence using each of these terms.

1. _____

2. _____

3. _____

I Complete each sentence with an appropriate vocabulary word or phrase from this unit. In many cases, more than one word or expression will work.

1. There are many ways in which people can steal your identity. Two of them are

_____ and _____.

2. A safe way to invest your money is by investing in _____.

3. A riskier way to invest is by investing in _____.

4. One good way to establish credit is _____.

5. Another way is _____.

6. If your identity is stolen, you should _____.

Research Project

A In the front of the phone book there is a section called the Blue Pages of Government Listings. These pages can help you find phone numbers of agencies that can give you financial help. Below are two of the best resources for financial help:

- FDIC (Federal Deposit Insurance Corporation)
  Consumers and Communities

- FTC (Federal Trade Commission)
  Consumer Protection

Discuss each of these agencies with your classmates and teacher.

1. What does the FDIC do? How can they help me?

2. What does the FTC do? How can they help me?

B To get more information about each of these agencies, go to their Web sites. Click on the topics you find interesting listed in the consumer section of each site. Write down what you find.

1. www.fdic.gov: _____

_____

_____

_____

2. www.ftc.gov: _____

_____

_____

_____

C Another Web site that has very useful information for consumers is www.consumeraction.gov. Go to the Web site and order a free copy of the *Consumer Action Handbook* online.

Free 2008 Consumer Action Handbook

Your new computer doesn't include a warranty. The sweater you ordered online never showed up. And the new washer you bought is noisy and leaking water. If you feel like you've just been ripped off, take action. Order your very own copy of the 2008 Consumer Action Handbook. You can expect your new Handbook to arrive within 4 weeks.

Team Project

Create a financial plan.

With a team, decide on one of these project options:

a. Create a financial plan for yourself. (one chart or poster per group member)

b. Create a financial plan for an imaginary person. (one chart or poster per group)

1. Form a team with four or five students. Choose positions for each member of your team.

POSITION	JOB DESCRIPTION	STUDENT NAME
Student 1: **Project Leader**	See that everyone speaks English. See that everyone participates.	
Student 2: **Secretary**	Take notes on team's ideas. Write a list of information that will go into financial plan.	
Student 3: **Designer**	Design financial plan.	
Student 4: **Spokesperson**	Report information to the class if team creates one plan for an imaginary person. Otherwise, assist team members with individual presentations.	
Student 5: **Assistant**	Help secretary and designer with their work.	

2. *Discuss and decide on what information should go in the financial plan: goals, organization templates for budget, plans for saving and reducing debt, names of investment vehicles, ways to protect against identity theft, and so on.

3. Organize the layout of the information for a poster.

4. Present the financial plan to the class.

* *Options:* If your team is creating individual financial plans, work together to decide what general information will go in each person's plan as well as how to organize the plans. Team members may then complete plans on their own.

Automotive Know-How

GOALS

➤ **Purchase a car**

➤ **Maintain and repair your car**

➤ **Interpret an auto insurance policy**

➤ **Compute mileage and gas consumption**

➤ **Follow the rules of the road**

Vocabulary Builder

Ⓐ Look at the different types of cars below. Use the terms in Exercise B to label the cars.

_____ _____ _____ _____ _____

_____ _____ _____ _____

Ⓑ How would you describe each car? Write your ideas next to each term below.

1. two-door coupe: _____

2. four-door sedan: _____

3. convertible: _____

4. minivan: _____

5. sport utility vehicle (SUV): _____

6. sports car: _____

7. station wagon: _____

8. pickup truck: _____

9. van: _____

C Below are some suggestions for car care that you will find in this unit. Read each suggestion and replace the verb in **bold** with a synonym from the box below. Some words can be used more than once.

change	do	look at
choose	find	replace
commute	imagine	fill up

1. _____ **Change** your air filter.

2. _____ **Check** your oil levels.

3. _____ **Drive** during off-peak hours.

4. _____ **Inspect** your brakes.

5. _____ **Look for** telecommuting opportunities.

6. _____ **Perform** an oil change.

7. _____ **Pick** your lane and stick with it.

8. _____ **Pretend** you're a hybrid.

9. _____ **Replace** your wipers today.

10. _____ **Top off** your washer fluid.

D What do the following words have in common? Write the theme below.

Theme: _____

_____ accident   _____ coverage   _____ make   _____ premium

_____ bodily injury   _____ incident   _____ model   _____ uninsured motorist

_____ collision   _____ limits of liability   _____ policy   _____ VIN

E Put a check (✔) next to the terms you know in Exercise D. Circle the ones you don't know. Walk around the classroom and talk to your classmates. Find people who know the terms you have circled.

Buying a car

GOAL ➤ **Purchase a car**

 A   In a group, discuss the following questions.

1. Do you have a car? (If not, think of someone you know who does.)
2. Describe the car. (Include color, size, make, model, etc.)
3. How did you get the car?
4. How long have you had it?

 B   Listen to an auto salesman who is trying to sell you a car. Take notes on what he says about the different kinds of cars.

CD
TR 14

Vehicle	Best for	Pros	Cons
	most people		
			backseats are hard to access
	active family		
		great in good weather	

C   Imagine you are going to buy a new or used car. Look back at the chart in Exercise B. Which kind of car would be best for you? _____

Why? _____

D   Now that you have an idea which car is best for you based on the salesman's descriptions, it is a good idea to do some research on your own. What are the best ways to find out more about the car you want to buy? In a group, brainstorm ways to research different car models.

Ways to Research the Car I Want to Buy

E   Rachel has decided to buy a car. She has been taking the bus and riding her bike everywhere so she has saved enough money to buy the car she wants. She has decided she wants a two-door coupe. Listen to what she did to research buying a car. Write down the different things she did.

CD
TR 15

1. _____

2. _____

3. _____

4. _____

5. _____

6. _____

F   To supplement your research, ask a variety of people for their opinions about cars. What are some questions you might ask? With a partner, create a list of questions.

Friends and Family

1._____

2._____

3._____

Car Dealer

1._____

2._____

3._____

Mechanic

1._____

2._____

3._____

Loan Officer

1._____

2._____

3._____

G   Create your plan to purchase a car. Write the steps you will take in the plan below.

My Car Purchase Plan
Step 1: _____ _____
Step 2: _____ _____
Step 3: _____ _____

Maintenance and repair

GOAL ➤ Maintain and repair your car

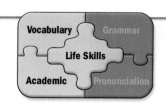

A With the help of your teacher, identify the auto parts below. Write the name of each part in the corresponding box.

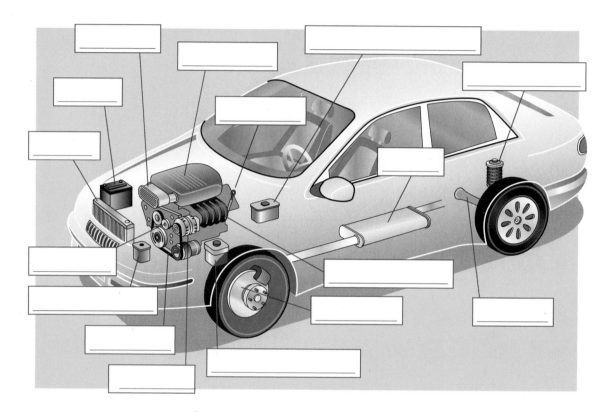

air filter	distributor	radiator
alternator	exhaust manifold	rear axle
battery	fuel injection system	rear suspension
brake fluid reservoir	muffler	timing belt
coolant reservoir	power steering reservoir	water pump
disc brake		

B What is the purpose of each part? Work with a partner and use a dictionary to define each part on a separate sheet of paper. Share your answers with other pairs.

C Now that you know about auto parts and their importance, read this excerpt from an auto maintenance and repair guide.

How to Maintain Your Automobile

Change your air filter. A clogged air filter can affect your gas mileage as well as the performance of your engine. Change it on a regular basis.

Check your oil levels. Your engine needs a certain amount of oil to run properly, so it's important to check the oil levels regularly.

Perform an oil change. As your engine uses oil, the oil becomes dirty and should be changed at regular intervals.

Perform a timing belt inspection. A faulty timing belt can result in bent valves and other expensive engine damage. Check it at least every 10,000 miles and replace it when the manufacturer recommends doing so.

Replace your wipers today. Windshield wipers can wear out, and if they aren't working properly, they could impair your vision while on the road. Change them at least twice a year.

Perform a radiator flush. It's important to keep your radiator and cooling system clean.

Check your power steering fluid. Check your power steering fluid regularly to make sure your power steering doesn't fail.

Inspect your brakes. Protect yourself and your passengers by inspecting your brakes twice a year.

Check and fill your coolant. If your car is low on coolant, it will run hot, so make sure to check the coolant level in your radiator.

Check and replace your spark plugs. A faulty spark plug could cause poor gas mileage and/or a rough running engine and poor acceleration. Make sure to replace the spark plugs as recommended by your car's manual.

Top off your washer fluid. Make sure you have enough washer fluid so you can keep your windshield clean.

Check your wheel bolts. Check the tightness of your wheel bolts on a regular basis to make sure there is no danger of your wheels becoming loose.

D With a partner, answer the following questions.

1. What fluids need to be regularly checked? (Hint: There are four.)

_____

2. Why is it important to replace windshield wipers?

_____

3. Why is it bad to have a clogged air filter?

_____

4. Why should you replace your timing belt?

_____

5. Why should you check your wheel bolts?

_____

6. What could happen if you don't have enough power steering fluid?

_____

E   Some people can perform their own maintenance while others need the help of trained professionals. Who will do your car repairs? If you need help, how will you go about finding a reliable mechanic and getting your repairs done? Read the guide below.

GUIDE TO GETTING REPAIRS DONE

1. Ask a friend, relative, or coworker for recommendations when looking for a good auto shop or mechanic. Also, take time to find a local garage that you feel comfortable with.
2. Make a list of services you need performed or the symptoms your vehicle is experiencing so there is no misunderstanding.
3. Get more than one opinion about the repairs that need to be done.
4. Ask for a written estimate before the job is started.
5. Get more than one estimate and compare prices.
6. Ask about the warranty policy.
7. Have the mechanic show you what you need replaced and have him explain why you need to replace it.
8. Go for a test drive in your car before paying for the repairs. If something is not right with the repairs, make it understood that you are not happy. Do not pay the bill until the vehicle is repaired properly.
9. Pay with a credit card. Many credit cards offer consumer protection for fraud.
10. If you discover something is not fixed after you've paid and driven home, call the garage and explain the situation. Go back to the garage as soon as possible.

F   Take out a piece of paper and number it from 1 to 10. Close your books and see how many suggestions from Exercise E you can remember. Write them down.

G   Make an outline for the two guides you read: one on maintaining your automobile and one on getting repairs done.

H   Using your outlines, write a two-paragraph summary of what you have learned in this lesson. Remember to include a topic sentence in each paragraph.

LESSON 3

Car insurance

GOAL ➤ **Interpret an auto insurance policy**

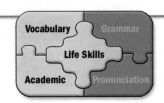

A Discuss these questions with your classmates.

1. Do you drive an automobile?
2. Do you have automobile insurance?
3. Why is it important to have auto insurance?
4. Do you understand your automobile insurance policy?
5. Is it against the law in your state to drive without insurance?

B Read what each person says about auto insurance policies. Look at Chalene's policy below.

"An insurance **policy** is a contract between you and the insurance company that states what the company will pay for in the event of an accident." — **Chalene**

"The insurance **premium** is the amount you pay for auto insurance for a certain period of time." — **Keona**

"**Coverage** is what is included in the insurance—what the company will pay for." — **Binata**

STANDOUT INSURANCE COMPANY

Name of Insured and Address	Policy Number:
Chalene Johnson 24573 Thatch Street Houston, TX 77042	05XX 52 87D 1625 Q **Policy Period:** Effective Jan 13, 2009 to Jul 13, 2009
Description of Vehicle(s) **Year and Make:** 2005 Acurak **VIN:** QXXPYR18924G23794	**Annual Mileage:** 9,000 **Premium for this Policy Period:** $212.38

Coverage	Limits of Liability	Six-Month Premium
A. Bodily Injury	Each Person $100,000; Each Accident $300,000	86.92
B. Collision	Each Accident $50,000	61.43
C. Comprehensive	Each Incident $25,000	36.04
D. Uninsured Motor Vehicle Bodily Injury	Each Person $50,000; Each Accident $150,000	27.99
	TOTAL	**$212.38**

C Look at Chalene's policy and find each of the items below.

1. Policy Number: _____

2. VIN: _____

3. Policy Premium: _____

4. Annual Mileage: _____

5. Length of Policy: _____

6. Make of Vehicle: _____

D   There are different types of coverage listed on insurance policies. Match each type of coverage with what it covers. Write the corresponding letter on the line.

Coverage	What it covers
1. bodily injury liability ____	a. other people's bodily injuries or death for which you are responsible
2. property damage liability ____	b. damage to another vehicle or property
3. collision ____	c. loss or damage to your vehicle or the vehicle you are driving for an incident other than collision (thievery, fire, etc.)
4. medical payments ____	d. damage to your vehicle due to an auto accident
5. comprehensive ____	e. bodily injuries to you or your passengers caused by the accident
6. uninsured motorist's bodily injury ____	f. bodily injury caused by another vehicle without insurance
7. uninsured motorist's property damage ____	g. damage caused by another vehicle without insurance

E   With a partner, read each scenario and decide which coverage would apply.

1. Chalene accidentally ran into a tree and damaged the front end of her car. Which coverage would apply? _____

2. Binata was driving home from school when she hit another car. She had run through a red light, so the accident was her fault. There was no real damage to her car, but she hurt her back and had to go to the chiropractor. Also, there was significant damage to the car she hit. Which types of coverage would apply? _____

3. Keona and his friend Chalene were driving to work when a car hit them from behind. Then the car drove off without giving them any information. Neither Keona nor Chalene was hurt, but there was damage to Keona's car. Which coverage would apply? _____

4. Keona's car got stolen from the parking lot at a movie theater. Which coverage would apply? _____

LESSON 3 GOAL ➤ Interpret an auto insurance policy

F Look back at Chalene's policy in Exercise B on page 53. Write a question for each answer.

EXAMPLE: Chalene Johnson: Who is being insured through this policy?

1. $61.43: _____

2. six months: _____

3. 05XX 52 87D 1625 Q: _____

4. 2005 Acurak: _____

5. $212.38: _____

6. 9,000: _____

G Look at Keona's insurance policy and answer the questions that follow.

United Automobile Association • Dallas, TX			
STATE: **TX** POLICY NUMBER: **QQP15 26 49L3798 1** POLICY PERIOD: **September 5, 2009 to March 5, 2010** VEHICLE(S): **2008 Fort Ficus, 2004 Chevnoret Tihoe**		NAME AND ADDRESS OF INSURED Keona Lu 54 Plover Plaza Galveston, TX 50472	
Limits of Liability			**6-Month Premium**
LIABILITY Bodily Injury Property Damage	Each Person $100,000; Each Accident $300,000 Each Accident $50,000		98.12 69.07
UNINSURED MOTORISTS Bodily Injury Property Damage	Each Person $100,000 Each Accident $300,000 Each Accident $50,000		27.00 21.45
PHYSICAL DAMAGE Comprehensive Loss Collision Loss	Deductible $1,000 Deductible $1,000		30.92 96.41
		TOTAL: $342.97	

1. How many vehicles are covered by this policy?
   a. 1   b. 2   c. 3   d. 4

2. Where does the insured motorist live?
   a. Dallas   b. Lake Tahoe   c. Galveston   d. Houston

3. How much is United Automobile Association charging for liability?
   a. $98.12   b. $69.07   c. $21.45   d. $167.19

4. What is Keona's deductible for comprehensive loss?
   a. $96.41   b. $30.92   c. $1,000   d. $50,000

Gas and mileage

GOAL ➤ **Compute mileage and gas consumption**

CD TR 16

A Read and listen to the conversation between Keona and Chalene.

Keona: I can't believe the price of gasoline! I've been spending almost $60 just to fill up my tank.

Chalene: Same here. I've been trying to figure out how I can use my car less, so I save some money on gas.

Keona: Any good ideas?

Chalene: Well, I'm going to start carpooling to school two days a week, which should help. And I'm trying to combine my errands so I only go out once a week.

Keona: That sounds good. I think I'm going to look into public transportation. I have a long drive to work so maybe I can figure out how to take the train into town. I'll have to drive to the station and park, but at least I won't be driving all the way to work.

Chalene: That's a great idea!

B Can you think of some other measures Keona and Chalene can take so they won't have to use their cars so much? Write your ideas below.

_____

_____

C Keona wanted to see how his gas mileage was so he started keeping track of his gas consumption and driving habits in a small notebook in his car. Look at a page from his book below.

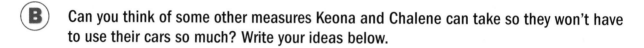

Date	Odometer	Trip	Gallons	MPG	Notes
8/7	12, 200	245 miles	13		a lot of street driving
8/15	12,475	275	14		highway driving
8/24	12,760	285	15		highway and street
9/1	13,020	260	14.5		

How do you think Keona might calculate his gas mileage in miles per gallon (MPG)? Create a formula and fill in the MPG column in the chart above.

GOAL ➤ **Compute mileage and gas consumption**

CD
TR 17

D In order to improve your gas mileage, you can follow certain maintenance tips. Listen and write the five tips you hear below.

Tips for improving gas mileage:

1. _____

2. _____

3. _____

4. _____

5. _____

E How will each of these tips help? Listen again and write the reasons on the lines below.

1. _____

2. _____

3. _____

4. _____

5. _____

F Keona followed these tips. Look at his log below and calculate the MPG and cost per mile. Did his MPG improve?

Date	Odometer	Trip	Gallons	MPG	Cost per gallon	Cost per mile
10/5	14,687	275 miles	13		$3.05	
10/17	14,962	295	14		$3.07	
10/30	15,262	300	15		$2.95	
11/9	15,542	280	14.5		$3.10	

Look at the cost per mile column. Which week was the cheapest? Come up with ideas how Keona can spend less per mile on gas.

G Here are some tips on how to change your driving habits in order to save gas.
In a small group, discuss each tip and figure out what it means.

1. No more drag racing.
2. Look farther down the road.
3. Pick your lane and stick with it.
4. Pretend you're a hybrid.
5. Carpool with classmates or coworkers.
6. Don't drive.
7. Drive during off-peak hours.
8. Look for telecommuting opportunities.

H Keona suggested that Chalene keep track of her gas consumption and mileage.
Fill in the missing numbers in her chart below.

Date	Odometer	Trip	Gallons	MPG	Cost per gallon	Cost per mile
10/5	22,758	310	15		$3.10	
10/20		325	16		$3.05	
10/30		320	15.5		$3.12	
11/12		280	17		$2.99	
11/18		275	16.5		$3.03	
AVERAGE						

I Think about your own driving habits (or traveling habits if you don't own a car). Fill in the chart
below as best you can and then make the calculations.

Date	Odometer	Trip	Gallons	MPG	Cost per gallon	Cost per mile

Traffic laws

GOAL ➤ **Follow the rules of the road**

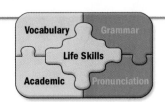

A What does each of the following signs mean? With a partner, see what you know.

_____

_____

_____

_____

_____

_____

_____

_____

_____

_____

_____

_____

_____

_____

_____

_____

B Think about the traffic laws you are familiar with. In a small group, write a law for each item.

EXAMPLE: yellow light: _You must slow down at a yellow light._

1. speed limit: _____

2. seat belts: _____

3. red light: _____

4. children: _____

5. pedestrians: _____

6. stop sign: _____

7. police officer: _____

8. school bus: _____

C Look back at the traffic laws you wrote for children and seat belts. The United States Department of Transportation has an organization called the National Highway Traffic Safety Administration (NHTSA) whose mission is to "save lives, prevent injuries, and reduce vehicle-related crashes." Read the data from a study NHTSA conducted and answer the questions that follow.

Occupant Fatalities in 2004 by Age and Restraint Use in Passenger Vehicles

Age group	Restrained	Percent restrained	Unrestrained	Percent unrestrained	Total	Total percent
<5	317	64	178	36	495	100
5–9	200	48	218	52	418	100
10–15	348	37	598	63	946	100
16–20	1,961	38	3,174	62	5,135	100
21–24	1,222	34	2,373	66	3,595	100
25–44	3,465	37	5,841	63	9,306	100
45–64	3,162	48	3,371	52	6,533	100
65–74	1,286	61	830	39	2,116	100
75+	2,117	69	958	31	3,075	100
Total	14,078	48	17,541	52	31,619	100

(*Source:* http://www.nhtsa.dot.gov)

1. What percentage of fatalities was unrestrained in the 21- to 24-year-old age group in 2004? _____

2. How many restrained 65- to 74-year-olds died in 2004? _____

3. How many children under age five died in 2004 because they weren't restrained? _____

4. What is the average percentage of unrestrained passengers who died in 2004? _____

5. How many adults over 44 died even though they were wearing seat belts? _____

D On a separate piece of paper write each question above as a statement.

EXAMPLE: Sixty-six percent of all vehicle fatalities involving 21- to 24-year-olds were unrestrained.

E What traffic law was violated by the unrestrained drivers and passengers? What law was violated by the parents of the unrestrained children?

F What are the driving laws regarding alcohol in your state? Discuss them with your class and write them below:

_____

_____

G Read the facts on alcohol-related accidents. Check (✔) the ones that are the most surprising to you.

☐ Alcohol-related motor vehicle crashes kill someone every 31 minutes and non-fatally injure someone every two minutes.

☐ In 2005, 16,885 people in the United States died in alcohol-related motor vehicle crashes, representing 39% of all traffic-related deaths.

☐ In 2005, nearly 1.4 million drivers were arrested for driving under the influence of alcohol or narcotics.

☐ Drugs other than alcohol (e.g., marijuana and cocaine) are involved in about 18% of motor vehicle driver deaths. These other drugs are generally used in combination with alcohol.

☐ More than half of the 414 child passengers ages 14 and younger who died in alcohol-related crashes during 2005 were riding with the drinking driver.

(*Source:* http://www.cdc.gov/ncipc/factsheets/drving.htm)

H With a partner, rewrite the facts above in your own words.

EXAMPLE: Someone is killed every half an hour due to a car accident involving
_____
alcohol.
_____

I In a small group, make a list of five driving rules that you all think are the most important. Present your list to the class.

_____

_____

_____

_____

_____

Review

(Lesson 1)

A List four different types of cars. (Lesson 1)

1. _____   3. _____

2. _____   4. _____

Which auto is best for you? _____   Why? _____

B Recall the auto maintenance tips you learned in Lesson 2. Write the correct verb from the box to complete each tip. You will need to use some of the verbs more than once. (Lesson 2)

| change | check | fill | inspect | perform | replace | top off |

1. _____ a radiator flush.
2. _____ your air filter.
3. _____ your washer fluid.
4. _____ your wipers today.
5. _____ your power steering fluid.
6. _____ your oil levels.
7. _____ an oil change.
8. _____ a timing belt inspection.
9. _____ your brakes.
10. _____ and _____ your coolant.
11. _____ your wheel bolts.

C Help Gary calculate his gas mileage and how much he is spending on gas. (Lesson 4)

Date	Odometer	Trip	Gallons	MPG	Cost per gallon	Cost per mile
2/7	46,269	310	15		$3.02	
2/17		325	16		$2.90	
2/28		320	15.5		$2.95	
3/5		280	17		$3.01	
AVERAGE						

How can Gary improve his gas mileage? With a partner, come up with five ways.

Read the insurance policy and answer the questions. (Lesson 3)

DriveRite Automotive Insurance Co., Inc.

Dung Nguyen 79563 Eastern Way Ambrose, GA 31512	Policy Number: QPX2 80 56 45F5542 6 Policy Period: 2/10/08-2/09/09	Vehicle: 2005 Folkswagin Passerine VIN: ZXYI493807T984XXX Annual Mileage: 12,500

Type of Coverage	Cost of Coverage	Limits of Liability	
A. Medical	$182.50	Each person Each accident	$100,000 $300,000
B. Liability	$175.00	Each person Each accident	$100,000 $300,000
C. Collision	$98.26	Each accident Each person	$50,000 $50,000
D. Uninsured motorist	$135.00	Each accident	$150,000
E. Comprehensive	$76.45	Each incident	$25,000

Premium: $667.21

1. Who is being insured through this insurance policy? _____

2. Where does the insured live? _____

3. How long is this policy in effect? _____

4. What is the total premium for Dung's policy? _____

5. How many miles does Dung drive per year? _____

6. Dung got in an accident last week, broke his leg, and damaged his car. Which types of coverage will pay for this? _____

7. How much is the insurance company charging for comprehensive coverage?
_____

8. If Dung's car gets stolen, how much will the insurance company pay to replace his car?
_____

9. What is the most the insurance company will pay for the property damage in an accident? _____

10. How much will the insurance company pay for each person who is hurt in an accident caused by someone without insurance? _____

On a separate piece of paper, write a summary about one of these topics. (Lessons 1-5)

- Purchasing a Car
- Maintaining a Car
- Saving Gas

- Keeping Track of Gas Mileage
- Auto Expenditures
- Rules of the Road

VOCABULARY REVIEW

F Write the name of each car part that has a box pointing to it.

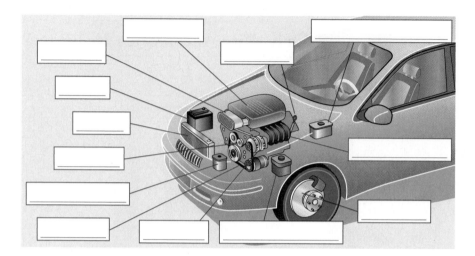

What does each part do? With a partner, take turns describing each part and its function.

G Write a defining sentence for each of the words below.

EXAMPLE: occupant: ___An occupant is a passenger in a car.___

1. premium: _____

2. collision: _____

3. MPG: _____

4. odometer: _____

5. fatalities: _____

6. unrestrained: _____

H Read each phrase below and match it with a vocabulary word or phrase from the unit.

EXAMPLE: restrains driver and/or passengers in an accident. ___seat belt___

1. identifies your vehicle: _____

2. covers damage to another vehicle: _____

3. can get clogged and affect your gas mileage: _____

4. tells you how fast you can drive on any given road: _____

5. the different things an insurance company will pay for: _____

6. tells you how many miles you have driven: _____

Research Project

A Searching the Internet is one of the easiest ways to find information. What key words would you use to search for the following services or offices? If you don't have access to the Internet, what headwords would you look under in a phone book to find the same information? Where else could you find the information? Work with a partner to complete the chart below.

Services/Offices	Internet key words	Phone book headwords	Other places to find information
Finding cars for sale			
Finding a mechanic			
Getting tips on how to maintain your car			
Getting auto insurance quotes from different companies			
Finding the local Department of Motor Vehicles (DMV)			
Finding out what the driving laws for your state are			

B Choose two of the items above that you want to do research on. How will you perform your research?

_____

What specific information are you looking for?

_____

C Conduct your research. What did you find? Write a summary of the information you collected.

_____

_____

_____

_____

_____

Team Project

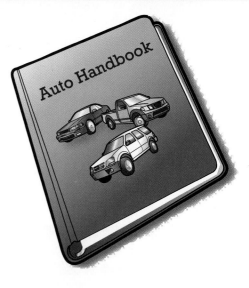

Create a class auto handbook.

With a team, you will create a section of an auto handbook. With the class, you will compile sections into a complete auto handbook.

1. Form a team with four or five students. Choose positions for each member of your team.

POSITION	JOB DESCRIPTION	STUDENT NAME
Student 1: **Project Leader**	See that everyone speaks English. See that everyone participates.	
Student 2: **Secretary**	Take notes on team's ideas.	
Student 3: **Designer**	Design layout of handbook section.	
Student 4: **Spokesperson**	Prepare team for presentation.	
Student 5: **Assistant**	Help secretary and designer with their work.	

2. As a class, brainstorm a list of topics to include in your auto handbook. You might include maintenance tips, directions on reading an insurance policy, and rules of the road. Count the number of teams and narrow your list of topics down to that number. Each team must choose a single topic to work on.

3. As a team, gather all the information for your group's section of the handbook.

4. Decide how you would like to present your information. You can choose pictures, lists of facts, and graphs. Be creative!

5. Create your section of the handbook.

6. Present your section of the handbook to the class.

7. Compile all the sections into one handbook.

Housing

GOALS

➤ **Communicate issues by phone**
➤ **Interpret rental agreements**
➤ **Identify tenant and landlord rights**

➤ **Get insurance**
➤ **Prevent theft**

Vocabulary Builder

A What do the following words have in common? Write the theme below.

Theme: _____

abandon	dwelling	grounds	summon
burglarize	enticing	premises	theft
crime	evident	responsible	thief
disturbance	exterior	seize	weapons

B Take each word and put it in the correct column according to its part of speech.
Use a dictionary if you need to.

Noun	Verb	Adjective

C Choose one word from each column in Exercise B. Write one sentence for each word.

1. _____

2. _____

3. _____

Vocabulary Builder

D Read.

> You can often tell the part of speech of a word just by looking at it. The following words are nouns. What do they have in common?
>
> prevention   installation   expiration
>
> The roots of these words are the verbs *prevent*, *install*, and *expire*. The suffix *-(a)tion* changes each verb into a noun. The noun form signifies the action or process of doing the action. For example, *prevention* signifies the action of preventing something.

E Following the examples in Exercise D, change each verb below into its noun form. Then, define each new word. Use your dictionary to check spelling.

Verb	Noun	Definition
1. activate	_____	_____
2. compensate	_____	_____
3. deteriorate	_____	_____
4. estimate	_____	_____
5. litigate	_____	_____
6. possess	_____	_____
7. terminate	_____	_____
8. vacate	_____	_____

F Without using a dictionary, try to match these phrases with their definitions.

_____ 1. fit for human occupancy   a. advance warning written in a business letter

_____ 2. formal written notice   b. estimate of how much one might pay for insurance

_____ 3. full compliance   c. being gone for a long time, longer than expected

_____ 4. housing codes   d. built well; a building in good condition

_____ 5. insurance quote   e. completely doing what you are required to do

_____ 6. prolonged absence   f. government regulations for building houses

_____ 7. replacement cost   g. government rules regarding health and cleanliness

_____ 8. sanitary regulations   h. suitable for people to live in

_____ 9. structurally sound   i. taking up a lot of time

_____ 10. time-consuming   j. the cost of replacing something

I have a problem.

GOAL ➤ **Communicate issues by phone**

 A Read and listen to the phone conversation Ming Mei is having with her landlord. What is the problem? How is the landlord going to fix it?

CD
TR 18

Landlord: Hello?

Ming Mei: Hi, Mr. Martin. This is Ming Mei from the apartment on Spring Street.

Landlord: Oh, hi, Ming Mei. What's up? Is there a problem?

Ming Mei: Well, after all the rain we had this weekend, the roof has started leaking. I think there may be a pool of water still on the roof because water is leaking through our ceiling even though the rain has stopped.

Landlord: Oh, no. Has it damaged the carpet?

Ming Mei: No, we caught it right away and put a bucket down to collect the drips.

Landlord: Oh, great. Thanks for being on top of it. I'll have my handyman come over and look at the roof and your ceiling. Can you let him in around ten this morning?

Ming Mei: I have to go to work, but I can get my sister to come over.

Landlord: Great. Thanks for calling, Ming Mei.

Ming Mei: Thank you, Mr. Martin.

B Practice the conversation with a partner. Switch roles.

 C Listen to the conversations between tenants and landlords. Take notes in the chart below.

CD
TR 19–21

	Problem	Solution
Conversation 1		
Conversation 2		
Conversation 3		

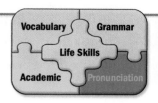

LESSON **1** **GOAL** ➤ **Communicate issues by phone**

D Look at the following statements from the conversation between Ming Mei and her landlord in Exercise A. Answer the questions.

I'll have my handyman come over and look at the roof and your ceiling.

1. Who is the subject of the sentence? _____

2. Who is going to come over? _____

I can get my sister to come over.

3. Who is the subject of the sentence? _____

4. Who is going to come over? _____

E The grammar in the two statements in Exercise D is called causative verb structure. We use this structure when we want to indicate that the subject causes something to happen. Study the chart with your teacher.

Causative Verbs: *Get, Have, Help, Make, Let*			
Subject	**Verb**	**Noun/Pronoun**	**Infinitive (Omit *to* except with *get*.)**
He	will get	his handyman	to come.
She	had	her mom	wait for the repairperson.
The landlord	helped	me	move in.
Ming Mei	makes	her sister	pay half of the rent.
Mr. Martin	let	Ming Mei	skip one month's rent.

F Match the causative verb from Exercise E with its meaning. Two verbs have the same meaning.

Verb

_____ 1. get

_____ 2. have

_____ 3. help

_____ 4. let

_____ 5. make

Meaning

a. allow

b. provide assistance

c. delegate responsibility to someone

d. require

GOAL ➤ **Communicate issues by phone**

G Unscramble the words and phrases to make causative statements. Then, write a housing-related sentence of your own using the same verb.

EXAMPLE: them / had / their landlord / and leave a deposit / fill out an application

Their landlord had them fill out an application and leave a deposit.

My landlord had me paint the apartment myself and he reimbursed me.

1. to prospective renters / him / let / the apartment / show / his tenants

_____

_____

2. made / my parents / a condo/ buy / me

_____

_____

3. my boss / for me / will get / I / to write / a letter of reference

_____

_____

4. her husband / she / which house to rent / decide / will let

_____

_____

5. find / my cousin / me / a new place to live / helped

_____

_____

H What should you do when you call your landlord? Read the list below.

1. State your name and where you live.
2. Clearly identify the problem.

3. Ask for a solution.
4. Restate the solution for clarification.

I What are some problems you might have with your home that would require you to call your landlord? Brainstorm a list on a separate piece of paper with a partner.

J With a partner, practice having phone conversations with a landlord. Use the problems you read in Exercise H and you wrote for Exercise I and come up with your own solutions.

Understand the fine print

GOAL ➤ Interpret rental agreements

A Have you ever rented a property? If so, do you remember what information was contained in your rental agreement? Make a list below.

<u>amount of rent</u>   _____   _____

_____   _____   _____

B Rental agreements are long and contain information to protect the tenant and the landlord. Much of the agreement is about money. Read the following money-related portion of a rental agreement.

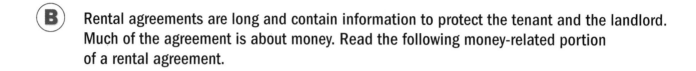

RENTAL AGREEMENT

RENT: To pay as rental the sum of $ _____ per month, due and payable in advance from the first day of every month. Failure to pay rent when due will result in the Owner taking immediate legal action to evict the Resident from the premises and seize the security deposit.

LATE FEE: Rent received after the first of the month will be subject to a late fee of 10% plus (3.00) dollars per day.

SECURITY DEPOSIT: Resident agrees to pay a deposit in the amount of $ _____ to secure Resident's pledge of full compliance with the terms of this agreement. The security deposit will be used at the end of the tenancy to compensate the Owner for any damages or unpaid rent or charges, and will be repaired at Resident's expense with funds other than the deposit.

RETURN OF DEPOSIT: Security deposits will be deposited for the Resident's benefit in a non-interest bearing bank account. Release of these deposits is subject to the provisions of State Statutes and as follows:

A. The full term of this agreement has been completed.

B. Formal written notice has been given.

C. No damage or deterioration to the premises, building(s), or grounds is evident.

D. The entire dwelling, appliance, closets, and cupboards, are clean and left free of insects; the refrigerator is defrosted; all debris and rubbish has been removed from the property; and the carpets are cleaned and left odorless.

E. Any and all unpaid charges, pet charges, late charges, extra visitor charges, delinquent rents, utility charges, etc., have been paid in full.

F. All keys have been returned, including keys to any new locks installed while Resident was in possession.

G. A forwarding address has been left with the Owner.

Thirty days after termination of occupancy, the Owner will send the balance of the deposit to the address provided by the Resident, payable to the signatories hereto, or the Owner will impose a claim on the deposit and so notify the Resident by certified letter. If such written claim is not sent, the Owner relinquishes his right to make any further claim on the deposit and must return it to the Resident provided Resident has given the Owner notice of intent to vacate, abandon, and terminate this agreement prior to the expiration of its full term, at least 7 days in advance.

C In a small group, interpret the money portion of the rental agreement. Underline things that no one in your group understands, so you can ask your teacher later.

D Read the sections on maintenance and repair.

RENTAL AGREEMENT

APPLIANCES: The above rental payment specifically EXCLUDES all appliances not permanently affixed. Appliances located at or in the property are there solely at the convenience of the Owner, who assumes no responsibility for their operation. In the event they fail to function after occupancy is started, the Resident may have them repaired at no cost to Owner or request Owner to remove them.

MAINTENANCE: Resident agrees to maintain the premises during the period of this agreement. This includes woodwork, floors, walls, furnishings and fixtures, appliances, windows, screen doors, lawns, landscaping, fences, plumbing, electrical, air-conditioning and heating, and mechanical systems. Tacks, nails, or other hangers nailed or screwed into the walls or ceilings will be removed at the termination of this agreement. Damage caused by rain, hail, or wind as a result of leaving windows or doors open, or damage caused by overflow of water, or stoppage of waste pipes, breakage of glass, damage to screens, deterioration of lawns and landscaping—whether caused by abuse or neglect—is the responsibility of the Resident.

RESIDENT'S OBLIGATIONS: The Resident agrees to meet all of Resident's obligations including:

A. Taking affirmative action to insure that nothing exists that might place the Owner in violation of applicable building, housing, and health codes.

B. Keeping the dwelling clean and sanitary; removing garbage and trash as they accumulate; maintaining plumbing in good working order to prevent stoppages and/or leakage of plumbing, fixtures, faucets, pipes, etc.

C. Operating all electrical, plumbing, sanitary, heating, ventilating, a/c, and other appliances in a reasonable and safe manner.

D. Assuring that property belonging to the Owner is safeguarded against damage, destruction, loss, removal, or theft.

REPAIRS: In the event repairs are needed beyond the competence of the Resident, he or she is urged to arrange for professional assistance. Residents are offered the discount as an incentive to make their own decisions on the property they live in. Therefore, as much as possible, the Resident should refrain from contacting the Owner except for emergencies or for repairs costing more than the discount since such involvement by the Owner will result in the loss of the discount. ANY REPAIR THAT WILL COST MORE THAN THE AMOUNT OF THE DISCOUNT MUST BE APPROVED BY THE OWNER OR THE TENANT WILL BE RESPONSIBLE FOR THE ENTIRE COST OF THAT REPAIR. Any improvement made by the tenant shall become the property of the Owner at the conclusion of this agreement.

WORKER'S WARRANTY: All parties to this agreement warrant that any work or repairs performed by the Resident will be undertaken only if he/she is competent and qualified to perform it, and the person performing the work will be totally responsible for all activities to assure they are done in a safe manner that will meet all applicable statutes. They further warrant that they will be accountable for any mishaps or accidents resulting from such work, and that they will hold the Owner free from harm, litigation, or claims of any other person.

E Divide into five groups. Each group will take one section from the rental agreement in Exercise D and become an "expert" on that section. Sections are marked by capital letters.

F Summarize your section for the class.

GOAL ➤ Interpret rental agreements

G Based on what you have read so far, what do you think the rental agreement will say about each of the following items? Write your ideas.

Gas, electric, and water: _____

Lead-based paint: _____

Phone: _____

Smoke detectors: _____

Utilities: _____

H Read the information taken from the rental agreement about the topics in Exercise G. Write the correct topic on the line that follows each section.

1. Resident agrees to install and maintain telephone service and agrees to furnish to the Owner the phone number, and any changes, within 3 days after installation.

   _____

2. Smoke detectors have been installed in this residence. It's the Resident's responsibility to maintain appliance including testing periodically and replacing batteries as recommended by the manufacturer. In the event the detector is missing or inoperative, the tenant has an affirmative duty to notify the landlord immediately.

   _____

3. Resident shall be responsible for payments of all utilities, garbage, water and sewer charges, telephone, gas, or other bills incurred during his/her residency. He/She specifically authorizes the Owner to deduct amounts of unpaid bills from their deposits in the event they remain unpaid after the termination of this agreement.

   _____

4. Resident agrees to transfer the gas, electric, and water service charges to their name immediately upon occupancy and to make arrangements for meter readings as needed.

   _____

5. Houses built before 1978 may contain lead-based paint. Lead from paint, paint chips, and dust can pose health hazards if not taken care of properly. Lead exposure is especially harmful to young children and pregnant women. Before renting pre-1978 housing, Owner must disclose the presence of known lead-based paint and lead-based paint hazards in the dwelling. Resident must also receive a federally approved pamphlet of lead-poisoning prevention.

   _____

I With a partner, go back through the three sections of the rental agreement provided in this lesson. Make a list of all the topics. (*Hint:* There are 14 topics.) Then, on a separate piece of paper, write a statement about each topic, summarizing what the rental agreement says about it.

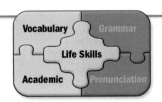

LESSON 3 — Your rights

GOAL ➤ **Identify tenant and landlord rights**

A Define the following terms with your teacher.

1. What is a *right*?

_____

2. What is a *responsibility*?

_____

B As a tenant, you have rights and responsibilities, just as your landlord does. Read the list below and indicate which responsibility belongs to each person: tenant (*T*) or landlord (*L*).

1. _____ Provide a clean apartment when the tenant moves in.

2. _____ Maintain common areas (hallways, stairs, yards, entryways).

3. _____ Give the landlord permission to enter the apartment at reasonable times and with advance notice to inspect it or to make any necessary repairs.

4. _____ Keep noise at a level that will not disturb neighbors.

5. _____ Keep the apartment and the surrounding area clean and in good condition.

6. _____ Notify the landlord immediately if the apartment needs repair through no fault of the tenant.

7. _____ Notify the landlord of any anticipated prolonged absence from the apartment so he or she can keep an eye on things.

8. _____ Pay the rent on time.

9. _____ Provide properly working plumbing and heating (both hot and cold running water).

10. _____ Repair any damage occurring to the apartment through the fault of the tenant, tenant's family members, or tenant's guests. Notify landlord at once of major damage.

11. _____ Provide well-lit hallways and entryways.

12. _____ When moving out, give landlord proper advance notice. Be sure that the apartment is in the same condition as when the tenant moved in and return the key to the landlord promptly.

C With a partner, restate each of the rights and responsibilities in Exercise B.

EXAMPLE: *"It is a landlord's responsibility to provide a clean apartment for the tenant. It is the tenant's right to have a clean apartment to move into."*

D Read about the implied warranty of habitability.

The "implied warranty of habitability" states that a landlord must keep the property in a condition fit for human occupancy. In other words, it must be a safe place for human beings to live in. Here are some questions a landlord might ask himself before he rents his property: Are there any known hazards with the property? Do the fixtures work properly? Is the building structurally sound? Does the property have any recurring problems?

If a landlord does not comply with the "implied warranty of habitability," a renter can cancel the lease, leave the premises, take the costs of repairs out of his rent, or ask for monetary damages.

In determining whether a landlord has violated the "implied warranty of habitability," courts will look at several factors:

1. Is the problem violating a housing code?
2. Is the problem violating a sanitary regulation?
3. Is the problem affecting a needed facility?
4. How long has the problem lasted?
5. How old is the building?
6. How much is the rent?
7. Has the tenant been ignoring the problem?
8. Is the tenant in any way responsible for the problem?

One or more of these factors will help the courts determine who is at fault and what the victim's rights may be.

E In a small group, discuss the following questions.

1. If your landlord violated the implied warranty of habitability, what would you do? Discuss each of the rights of a renter listed above and decide what you would do. Take notes.

_____

_____

2. According to the list of questions that courts will ask, what are some situations in which you could take a landlord to court?

_____

_____

3. Discuss some situations when you couldn't take a landlord to court. Take notes.

_____

_____

F With a partner, look at each picture below. Decide if it violates the implied warranty of habitability. Imagine that each of these situations has gone on for at least three weeks with no response from the landlord.

G Imagine that you are a landlord. Use the rights and responsibilities in Exercise B to write four statements using a causative verb structure.

EXAMPLE: _The law makes me provide a clean apartment for the tenant._

1. _____

2. _____

3. _____

4. _____

H Imagine that you are a tenant. Look back at the rights and responsibilities in Exercise B. Write four statements using a causative verb structure.

EXAMPLE: _The law makes me pay the rent on time._

1. _____

2. _____

3. _____

4. _____

Insuring your home

GOAL ➤ Get insurance

  A Listen to Makela and Bryce talk about the renter's insurance quote below.

CD
TR 22

Renter's Insurance Quote	
Value of Personal Property	$29,000
Deductible	$250
Liability	$100,000
Medical Payments	$1,000
Annual Premium	$220.08
Monthly Payment	$18.34

B Discuss the following questions with your classmates.

1. Do you have insurance for your property? Why or why not?
2. What is a deductible? What is Makela's deductible?
3. What is the liability insurance for?
4. What are the medical payments for?
5. What will Makela pay per year for renter's insurance?

C What is the value of your personal property? Write the estimated replacement costs below.

Personal property	Typical replacement cost	Your estimated replacement cost
Personal Computer, Accessories, and Software	$1,500–$4,000	
TV and Stereo Equipment (Home and Portable)	$500–$4,000	
Music and Movie Collection	$500–$2,000	
Furniture and Household Items	$5,000–$15,000	
Clothing and Shoes	$2,000–$4,000	
Sporting Goods	$500–$2,000	
Camera and Video Equipment	$200–$1,000	
Jewelry and Watches	$1,000	
Other (Luggage, Tools, etc.)	$1,000–$3,000	
Total Estimated Replacement Costs		

D Landlords should carry insurance for the structures they rent to others. Imagine that you own your own property. Then, imagine that you rent the same space from a landlord. How do you think homeowner's insurance is different from renter's insurance?

E Read the Hahn's homeowner's insurance policy below. Then, answer the questions that follow.

State One Insurance

Name/Address of Insured: Steve and Rosemary Hahn
7930 Inca Way, Kansas City, MO 64108

Deductible: $2,500	Annual Premium: $1,077.93
Coverage Type	**Amount of Coverage**
Dwelling	$401,000
Personal Property	$300,750
Loss of Use	$80,200
Personal Liability—Each Occurrence	$100,000
Medical Payments to Others—Each Person	$1,000

1. How much will the insurance company pay to rebuild the house? _____

2. How much will the insurance company pay to replace personal belongings? _____

3. How much will the family have to pay before the insurance company pays? _____

4. What is the monthly premium? _____

F To get homeowner's insurance, the insurance company needs information about your building. Read about the Hahn's home. Then, fill in the information about your home.

Building feature	Hahn's home	My home
Year Built	1986	
Total Square Footage	2,378 sq. ft.	
Number of Stories	2	
Exterior Wall Construction Material	stucco on frame	
Roof Type	clay tile	
Garage or Carport	attached garage: 2-car	
Wall Partitions Construction Materials	drywall	
Wall / Floor Covering Materials	paint / wood and tile	
Number of Kitchens / Bathrooms	1 / 3	
Type of Air / Heat	central air / gas	

Vocabulary | Grammar
Life Skills
Academic | Pronunciation

G I HAVE INSURANCE. If you already have insurance, think about your own answers to the questions below. See possible answers in parentheses.

1. What type of policy do you have? (homeowner's, renter's) _____

2. How long have you had your policy? (six months, two years, ten years) _____

3. What is your monthly premium? ($45, $82, $150) _____

4. How often do you review your policy in case changes need to be made? (every 3 months, once a year, never) _____

I DON'T HAVE INSURANCE. If you *don't* have insurance for your property, think about your answers to the questions below. See some possible answers in parentheses.

1. What type of policy do you need? (homeowner's, renter's) _____

2. How can you find an insurance company? (ask a friend or family member, search online, look in the phone book) _____

3. How much personal property coverage do you need? ($5,000, $17,000, $50,000)

_____

4. How much can you spend per month on insurance? ($50, $100, $150) _____

H Using the questions in Exercise G, interview three classmates. Take notes about your interviews. Interviewees can use their own answers or choose one from the examples in parentheses.

Name: _____ Insurance (yes/no) Type: _____

Notes: _____

Name: _____ Insurance (yes/no) Type: _____

Notes: _____

Name: _____ Insurance (yes/no) Type: _____

Notes: _____

I Write a statement about what you are going to do this week to protect yourself.

EXAMPLE: _I need renter's insurance for my personal property. This week, I'm going to go online and get quotes from three insurance companies._

Protecting your home

GOAL ➤ **Prevent theft**

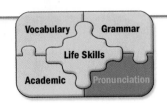

A Use a dictionary to define the words below. Include the part of speech for each word. Then, answer the questions that follow.

burglar: _____

burglarize: _____

burglary: _____

burgle: _____

theft: _____

thief: _____

thieve: _____

1. What is the difference between the two sets of words? _____

_____

2. There are two pairs of synonyms in the groups of words above. What are they?

_____ and _____   _____ and _____

B You are about to read a newsletter on how to protect your home from being burglarized. What do you predict it will say about the following items? Brainstorm with a group.

Light	Time	Noise

LESSON 5   **GOAL** ➤ **Prevent theft**

Vocabulary   Grammar
Life Skills
Academic   Pronunciation

C   Read.

Theft Prevention Newsletter

Burglary Prevention

Each year in the United States, there are more than five million home burglaries. Nine out of ten of these crimes are preventable. The risk of being burglarized can be greatly reduced by taking simple steps to make your home more difficult to enter and less enticing to would-be burglars. **Remember the greatest weapons in the fight to prevent burglaries are light, time, and noise.**

(Source: http://www.jcsd.org/burglary_prevention.htm)

LIGHT

- Make sure that exterior lights are mounted out of reach so that burglars can't easily unscrew bulbs.
- Consider buying motion-sensitive lights, which are now available at relatively low prices.
- Use a variable light timer to activate lights inside your home.
- Trim trees and shrubs near doors and windows so burglars can't hide in the shadows.

TIME

Make it time-consuming for a burglar to break into your home by:

✓ installing deadbolt locks on all exterior doors.

✓ installing double key locks in doors that contain glass. This will keep a burglar from being able to open the door simply by breaking the glass and reaching through. *(Note: So that everyone in the house can get out in the event of a fire, be sure to keep the key in a designated place.)*

✓ placing additional locks on all windows and patio doors.

NOISE

- Get a dog. You don't need a large attack dog; even a small dog creates a disturbance that burglars would prefer to avoid. Remember to license and vaccinate it.
- Consider having someone care for your dogs in your home while you're away instead of boarding them.
- If you can afford it, install an alarm system that will alert neighbors of a burglar's presence. Most systems can even summon local police directly.

D   Compare the ideas you brainstormed in Exercise B to the tips from the newsletter. Are there any tips you didn't think of? List them in the chart.

Light	Time	Noise

  E

CD
TR 23

Listen to the police officer talk about other tips to prevent break-ins. Write the tips below.

Other tips to prevent break-ins:

1. _____
2. _____
3. _____
4. _____
5. _____
6. _____

  F

CD
TR 24

Sometimes, all your efforts will not stop a determined burglar. It is wise to take some precautions that will help you get your property back should a criminal successfully break into your home. Listen to the police officer and take notes.

1. _____
2. _____
3. _____
4. _____
5. _____
6. _____

G Make a flier to post in your community. Include the most important tips you learned about how to prevent theft in your home.

Review

A With a partner, practice conversations between a tenant and a landlord. Practice both face-to-face and phone conversations. Use the scenarios below. (Lesson 1)

1. leaky faucet

2. broken window

3. can't pay rent on time this month

4. noisy neighbors

B Using the words provided below, write complete sentences using the causative verb structure. You may choose the verb tense to use. (Lesson 1)

EXAMPLE: she / make / her sister / move

<u>She made her sister move out of her apartment.</u>

1. I / get / her / meet

_____

2. they / have / their friends / wait

_____

3. Elliot / help / his father / repair

_____

4. my father / make / me / pay

_____

5. his landlord / let / him / fix

_____

C Make a list of five topics that can be found in a rental agreement. After each topic, write a typical statement that might be found in such an agreement. (Lesson 2)

EXAMPLE: <u>Rent: The rent must be paid on the first day of each month.</u>

1. _____

2. _____

3. _____

4. _____

5. _____

D Identify three rights that a tenant and landlord have by writing them on the lines below. (Lesson 3)

Tenant's Rights

1. A tenant has the right to _____.

2. _____

3. _____

Landlord's Rights

1. A landlord has the right to _____.

2. _____

3. _____

E Read the insurance policy and answer the questions. (Lesson 4)

INSURANCE POLICY

Deductible:	****$2,250.00****	Annual Premium:	****$989.45****

Coverage Type	Amount of Coverage
Dwelling	******$330,000
Loss of Use	*******$80,200
Medical Payments to Others—Each Person	********$1,000
Personal Liability—Each Occurrence	******$100,000
Personal Property	******$200,000

1. Is this a homeowner's or renter's policy? _____

   How do you know? _____

2. How much will the insurance company pay to rebuild the house? _____

3. What is the annual premium? _____

4. How much will the insurance company pay to replace personal belongings?

   _____

F Write *T* (true) or *F* (false) in front of each theft prevention tip. (Lesson 5)

_____ 1. Place your valuables in easy-to-see locations.

_____ 2. Lock up anything that could be used to break into your house.

_____ 3. Install an alarm system.

_____ 4. Make sure you turn off all the lights when you leave your home.

_____ 5. Install double key locks on all your windows.

_____ 6. Let your neighbors know when you will be out of town.

VOCABULARY REVIEW

G Complete each question with a word or phrase from this unit. There may be more than one correct answer.

1. Have you ever been _____?

2. How much _____ do you have for your personal property?

3. Do you have _____ or _____ insurance?

4. What is your monthly _____?

5. Do you have _____ installed in your house?

6. What would your landlord do if there were a _____ in your building?

H With a partner, ask and answer the questions in Exercise G.

I Without using a dictionary, define the following words. Include the part of speech.

1. dwelling: _____

2. policy: _____

3. right: _____

4. burglary: _____

5. responsibility: _____

6. prevent: _____

7. vacate: _____

8. premium: _____

J With a partner, write a conversation on a separate piece of paper using as many of the words from Exercise I as you can include.

Research Project

A All of the information you find on the Internet may not be reliable. Imagine you are searching for more information about what you have learned in this unit (tenant rights, preventing theft, rental agreements, etc.). Which Web address endings below do you think contain the most reliable information? Circle your answers.

.com   .net   .org   .biz   .edu   .gov   .us   .tv

B If you don't have access to the Internet, but you want to find out more about the following topics, where would you look for reliable information?

Tenant Rights: _____

Renter's Insurance: _____

Homeowner's Insurance: _____

Rental Agreements: _____

Theft Prevention: _____

Reporting a Burglary: _____

C Choose one of the topics from Exercise B. Conduct research using any method you have access to, including the Internet, people you know, and local sources. Then, answer the questions below.

1. Which topic did you research?_____

2. Where did you find your research (specific source)? _____

_____

3. How do you know this is a reliable source? _____

_____

4. What information did you find? _____

_____

_____

_____

_____

_____

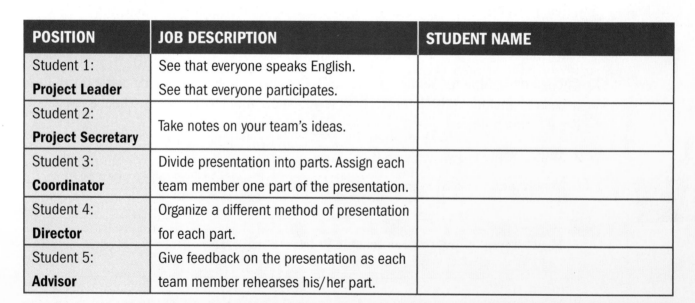

Make a presentation related to housing issues.

Presentation Topics

- Communication with a Landlord or Tenant
- Rental Agreements
- Tenant and Landlord Rights
- Renter's or Homeowner's Insurance
- Theft Prevention

1. Form a team with four or five students. Decide which topic your team will work on. (Each team should choose a different topic from the list above.)

2. Choose positions for each member of your team.

POSITION	JOB DESCRIPTION	STUDENT NAME
Student 1: **Project Leader**	See that everyone speaks English. See that everyone participates.	
Student 2: **Project Secretary**	Take notes on your team's ideas.	
Student 3: **Coordinator**	Divide presentation into parts. Assign each team member one part of the presentation.	
Student 4: **Director**	Organize a different method of presentation for each part.	
Student 5: **Advisor**	Give feedback on the presentation as each team member rehearses his/her part.	

3. Gather the information for your presentation.

4. Decide how to present your information to the class. For example, you may want to use charts, skits, or games.

5. Create any materials needed for your presentation.

6. Rehearse your presentation.

7. Give your presentation to the class.

Health

GOALS

➤ **Identify practices that promote mental and physical well-being**

➤ **Ask about medical bills**

➤ **Interpret health insurance information**

➤ **Identify addictions**

➤ **Interpret procedures for first aid**

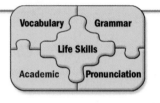

Vocabulary Builder

A A *word family* is a group of words with the same root. The words all have similar meanings but are used as different parts of speech. Look at this example.

Noun(s)	Verb	Adjective
survival, survivor	survive	surviving

- There were no *survivors* from the car accident.
- If cancer is detected early, there is a good chance of *survival*.
- Drugs that dissolve blood clots can help people *survive* heart attacks.
- The *surviving* passengers from the plane crash tried to find help.

B Put the words below into the correct column in the chart. Then, use your dictionary to find the other forms of each word family. *Note:* Not every word family has every part of speech.

> ~~affecting~~   withdrawal   poisoning   depressed   tolerance
> impairment   addiction   meditate   insured   treat

Noun	Verb	Adjective	Adverb
affect	affecting, affect, affected	affecting, affective	

Noun	Verb	Adjective	Adverb

C Choose one of the word families from Exercise B that has all four parts of speech. Write a sentence using each word form. Use the example sentences in Exercise A as a model.

1. _____

2. _____

3. _____

4. _____

D Each expression below is related to health. What do you think each one means? Write your ideas on the lines.

1. mental health: _____

2. out of shape: _____

3. self-esteem: _____

4. at risk: _____

E Look at the following questions. Answer the ones you feel comfortable answering.

1. What are the major health-care issues facing your community? Which health-care issues can be categorized as mental-health issues?

_____

2. Do you consider yourself in good shape? Why or why not?

_____

3. Think about people who have high self-esteem. What are their traits? What are the traits of people with low self-esteem?

_____

4. Do you know your family's health history? If so, what problems have faced some of your family members?

_____

LESSON **1**

Mind and body

GOAL ➤ **Identify practices that promote mental and physical well-being**

 A Discuss the following questions with a small group.

1. Do you exercise? If so, what type of exercise do you do and how often?

2. Do you eat well? On a scale of one to ten (ten being the healthiest), how healthy are the foods you eat?

3. How could you make your diet healthier?

4. How much water do you drink a day?

5. Do you have a lot of stress in your life? How do you relieve stress?

 B Listen to the following people talk about how they handle stress. Take notes.

CD
TR 25

Cooper

Stephanie

Fletcher and Katie

Reason for stress:

_____

How he copes with
his stress:

_____

_____

Reason for stress:

_____

How she copes with
her stress:

_____

_____

Reason for stress:

_____

How they cope with
their stress:

_____

_____

C Do you identify with any of these people? If yes, in what ways? If not, why not?

D "Dear Ali" is a column in the local newspaper. Ali addresses health issues. Read her column. Do you agree with her advice?

Daily Freepress News

1. Dear Ali,
I don't look forward to getting out of bed in the morning. I don't like my job. I don't like to go to school. I don't have any family around and I have very few friends. I feel like there is no reason to get up in the morning. **—Unhappy**

Dear Unhappy,
You are depressed. But that doesn't mean you can stay in bed forever. Do things that will make you want to get out of bed. Take a nice hot shower. Go for a walk. Drink some water. Eat some fresh fruit. Find something that you can look forward to. Every day, add one more thing to your day that you enjoy

doing. If you don't like your job, look for a new one. Find some classes at a nearby school that you like. Remember, we don't always like everything that we have to do in life to survive. But, if you can fill your day with at least one or two things that make you happy, it will make the rest of your day liveable.

2. Dear Ali,
I'm overweight and out of shape. I can't bear to look at myself in the mirror, and it is really affecting my self-esteem. What can I do?
—Overweight & Out of Shape

Dear Overweight & Out of Shape,
There are only two things I can say . . . diet and exercise! The only way to lose weight and keep it off is to eat a healthy, low-calorie diet and exercise. If you can't do it by yourself, find a friend or family member to do it with you or join one of the many weight-loss programs out there. You can do it!

E Pretend you are Ali and give advice to the following concerned people.

Dear Ali,
My daughter is overweight. All of the kids make fun of her at school, and I think she eats even more because she is unhappy. I try to cook healthy food at home but that doesn't seem to be helping. What can I do?
—*Mother Without a Clue*

_____

_____

_____

Dear Ali,
I have a lot of stress at work. My boss pushes me pretty hard, and I want to do a good job to get ahead, but I never have any time for myself or for my family. The doctor says all the stress is giving me high blood pressure. What should I do?—*Overworked*

_____

_____

_____

GOAL ➤ **Identify practices that promote mental and physical well-being**

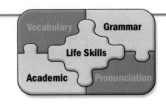

 F Danielle wrote a health-related article for her school paper. Read her article.

BACK ON TRACK

I think I take pretty good care of myself. But it wasn't always that way. I used to work really long hours, eat at fast-food restaurants because they were quick and easy, and I barely ever exercised. But I got a wake-up call from the doctor one day. He said I was obese and at risk for diabetes and that I might not make it to my fortieth birthday. From that day forward, I began to make changes in my life. I started by going for a walk every day. Now I go to the gym three times a week, walk six miles two days a week, and play volleyball with my family on the weekends. The day the doctor gave me that horrible prognosis, I went straight to the market and filled my cart with healthy food. I now make my lunch every day and cook healthy dinners for my family. My purse and my car are always filled with healthy snacks and water. If I ever get a craving for something really unhealthy, I let myself have one bite of it, and then I stick a piece of gum in my mouth. Although the exercise and eating habits really helped to lower my blood pressure and risk for diabetes, I still have quite a bit of stress in my life. To combat that, I make sure I take at least a half an hour a day for myself. Sometimes I meditate, sometimes I call a good friend, and other times I just sit down and read a book for pleasure.

G Answer the following questions.

1. What forced Danielle to make changes in her life?

2. What changes did she make?

3. Do you think her article is inspiring? Why or why not?

H With your classmates, create a health newsletter. Follow the steps below.

1. Each student writes a health article that will be inspiring to others who read it.

2. After everyone has finished his or her article, work together to edit the articles.

3. Come up with a title for your newsletter.

4. Put your newsletter together. Add artwork or photos if you want.

What's this charge for?

GOAL ➤ Ask about medical bills

Vocabulary | Grammar
Life Skills
Academic | Pronunciation

  A Listen to the phone conversation Mrs. Gregory is having with the doctor's office.

CD
TR 26

DOCTOR	Statement Date:	10/06/2008

DOCTOR
Amy Rosenberg, M.D., Inc.
2880 Chestnut Ave., Ste. 340
Topeka, KS 66675
Office Phone (785) 555-0012

Statement Date:	10/06/2008
Statement #:	4689-36
Balance Due:	$20.00

RESPONSIBLE PARTY
Mrs. Linda Gregory
56 Plains Ave.
Topeka, KS 66675

MAKE CHECK PAYABLE AND REMIT TO
Amy Rosenberg, M.D., Inc.
2880 Chestnut Ave., Ste. 340
Topeka, KS 66675

PATIENT NAME: Gregory, Courtney   **PROVIDER:** Rosenberg, M.D., Amy

Date	Procedure	Description of Service	Co-Pay	Amount Payable
8/23/2008	99391	Well-Child Check		$100.00
8/23/2008	90700	DTaP Vaccine		$40.00
8/23/2008	90465	Vaccine Admin		$28.00
8/23/2008	90645	Hib Vaccine		$32.00
8/23/2008	90466	Vaccine Admin		$28.00
8/23/2008		Patient Co-Pay	-$20.00	
9/01/2008		Primary Insurance Payment		-$120.00
9/01/2008		Uncollectible		-$68.00

B Answer the questions.

1. Who is expected to pay this bill?

2. Why did Courtney go to the doctor?

3. Why is the responsible party different from the patient's name?

4. How much is owed?

5. Why is the responsible party confused about the amount she owes?

6. Does anything on the bill confuse you? Write a question about something you don't understand.

LESSON **2** **GOAL** ➤ **Ask about medical bills**

CD
TR 27

C Read and listen to the following conversation between a patient and the doctor's office.

Receptionist: Dr. Brook's office.

Patient: Um, yes, this is Cooper Jackson. I came in and saw the doctor a few months ago for the pain I was having in my leg. I just received the bill and I have a few questions.

Receptionist: Of course, Mr. Jackson. Let me pull up your records. Do you have the date of the statement?

Patient: Yes, it is June 16th.

Receptionist: Ok, I have it here. How can I help you?

Patient: Well, I don't understand what this $264 charge is for.

Receptionist: That is for the X-rays the technician took of your leg.

Patient: OK, but shouldn't my insurance pay for that?

Receptionist: Yes, they might pay some. As you can see on the bill, we have billed your insurance company but are still waiting to hear back from them. Once we do, we'll send you an adjusted bill reflecting how much you owe.

Patient: Oh, so if I don't have to pay this $264, why did you send me a bill?

Receptionist: I know it may seem a bit confusing. Our billing department automatically sends out statements to our current patients every month, whether or not we have heard back from the insurance companies. It usually takes about a month for the bill to reflect what the insurance company has paid, so, in general, if you wait two or three months to pay your bill, your statement should show the correct amount due.

Patient: I see. That makes sense. So, I don't need to pay this bill now?

Receptionist: No. Wait until you receive a bill with an adjusted amount on it and then send in your payment.

Patient: Great! Thanks for your help.

Receptionist: Have a nice day, Mr. Jackson.

D Practice the conversation with a partner. Switch roles.

E Practice the conversation again. This time use the information below to change the patient's questions. The receptionist will have to be creative to come up with a response.

Name	Reason for visit	Date of statement	Question
Jenna Lyn	toothache	May 25	Why isn't the payment I made showing up on the statement?
Javier Bardo	headaches	December 2	Do you offer discounted services? I don't have health insurance.
Kim Jensen	skin rash	March 14	Why do I have to pay more than my co-pay?
Young Lee	ingrown toenail	July 7	Why didn't my insurance pay for the procedure?

GOAL ➤ **Ask about medical bills**

F Look at the bill below. Write five questions you would ask someone at the doctor's office.

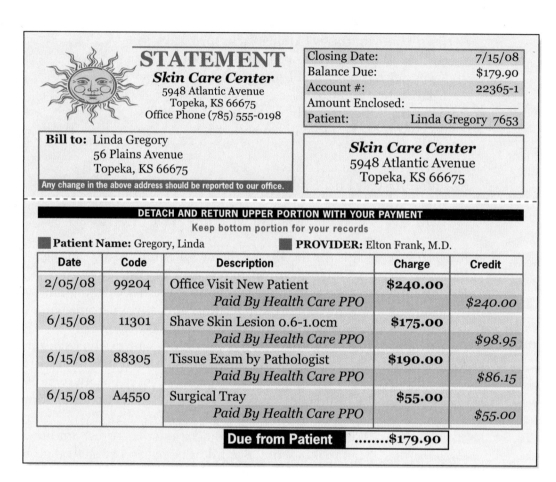

STATEMENT
Skin Care Center
5948 Atlantic Avenue
Topeka, KS 66675
Office Phone (785) 555-0198

Closing Date:	7/15/08
Balance Due:	$179.90
Account #:	22365-1
Amount Enclosed:	
Patient:	Linda Gregory 7653

Bill to: Linda Gregory
56 Plains Avenue
Topeka, KS 66675
Any change in the above address should be reported to our office.

Skin Care Center
5948 Atlantic Avenue
Topeka, KS 66675

DETACH AND RETURN UPPER PORTION WITH YOUR PAYMENT
Keep bottom portion for your records

Patient Name: Gregory, Linda   **PROVIDER:** Elton Frank, M.D.

Date	Code	Description	Charge	Credit
2/05/08	99204	Office Visit New Patient	$240.00	
		Paid By Health Care PPO		$240.00
6/15/08	11301	Shave Skin Lesion 0.6-1.0cm	$175.00	
		Paid By Health Care PPO		$98.95
6/15/08	88305	Tissue Exam by Pathologist	$190.00	
		Paid By Health Care PPO		$86.15
6/15/08	A4550	Surgical Tray	$55.00	
		Paid By Health Care PPO		$55.00

Due from Patient $179.90

1. _____

2. _____

3. _____

4. _____

5. _____

G Go over the bill with your teacher to make sure you understand everything on it.

H Find a partner (receptionist) and have a conversation, asking him or her the questions you wrote above. Switch roles.

Health insurance

GOAL ➤ Interpret health insurance information

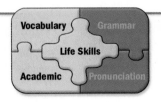

A What do you know about health insurance? In a small group, try to answer the following questions. If you need more help, talk to other groups.

1. Is it mandatory in your state to have health insurance?
2. What happens if you go to the doctor's or hospital without health insurance?
3. What is the difference between an HMO and a PPO?
4. Name four health insurance companies.

B Read the bar graph about the insured and uninsured and answer the questions.

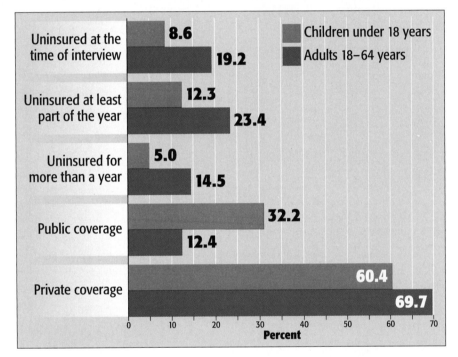

Percentage of persons without health insurance, by three measurements and age group, and percentage of persons with health insurance, by coverage type and age group: United States, January, 2007–June, 2007

(*Source:* Family Core component of the 2007 National Health Interview Survey. The estimates for 2007 are based on data collected January through June. Data are based on household interviews of a sample of the civilian non-institutionalized population.)

1. What percentage of adults is insured?
2. Of the uninsured people, what percentage of children was uninsured for more than a year?
3. What percentage of adults has private insurance?
4. What percentage of children has public coverage?

C Ask your partner questions about the information presented in the graph. Use the questions from Exercise B as examples.

D **Read the graph and complete the sentences below.**

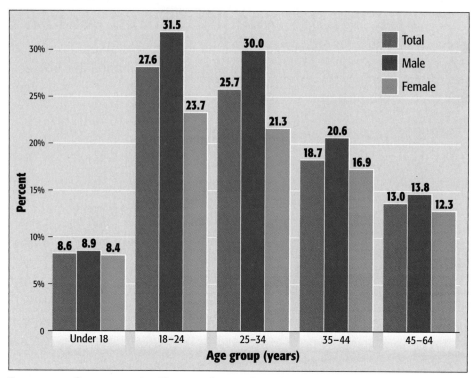

Percentage of persons under 65 years of age without health insurance coverage at the time of interview, by age group and sex: United States, January, 2007–June, 2007

(*Source:* Family Core component of the 2007 National Health Interview Survey. The estimates for 2007 are based on data collected January through June. Data are based on household interviews of a sample of the civilian non-institutionalized population.)

1. Of both sexes, the _____ are the most uninsured.

2. Out of all the age groups, the _____ -year-olds are the most uninsured.

3. _____ of children are uninsured.

4. _____ of children are insured.

5. _____ of women ages 35–44 are uninsured.

6. _____ of people in my age group are uninsured.

E **Write three more sentences about the statistics in the graph.**

1. _____

2. _____

3. _____

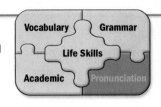
F   Look at the data in the table below and write six questions based on the data.

Selected characteristic	Uninsured[1] at the time of interview	Uninsured[1] for at least part of the year[2]	Uninsured[1] for more than a year[2]
RACE/ETHNICITY	**PERCENT** *(standard error)*		
Hispanic or Latino	**31.4** *(1.11)*	**35.6** *(1.17)*	**25.8** *(1.08)*
Non-Hispanic			
White, single race	**10.2** *(0.37)*	**13.7** *(0.42)*	**7.1** *(0.31)*
Black, single race	**14.4** *(0.65)*	**17.8** *(0.74)*	**9.6** *(0.57)*
Asian, single race	**13.0** *(1.57)*	**15.7** *(1.71)*	**9.4** *(1.26)*
Other races & multiple races	**23.6** *(4.52)*	**28.8** *(4.26)*	**11.3** *(1.84)*
EDUCATION[3]			
Less than high school	**31.2** *(1.06)*	**35.1** *(1.10)*	**26.1** *(1.07)*
High school diploma or GED[4]	**19.1** *(0.55)*	**22.3** *(0.60)*	**14.8** *(0.50)*
More than high school	**10.4** *(0.36)*	**14.3** *(0.41)*	**7.0** *(0.29)*
EMPLOYMENT STATUS[5]			
Employed	**17.9** *(0.48)*	**22.3** *(0.52)*	**13.8** *(0.45)*
Unemployed	**47.4** *(2.16)*	**51.8** *(2.11)*	**33.5** *(2.06)*
Not in workforce	**19.9** *(0.77)*	**23.6** *(0.83)*	**14.5** *(0.62)*

Percentage of persons who lacked health insurance coverage at the time of interview, for at least part of the past year, or for more than a year, by selected demographic characteristics: United States, January, 2007–June, 2007.

[1] A person was defined as uninsured if he or she did not have any private health insurance, Medicare, Medicaid, State Children's Health Insurance Program (SCHIP), state-sponsored or other government-sponsored health plan, or military plan.

[2] A year is defined as the 12 months prior to interview.

[3] Education and marital status are shown only for persons aged 18 years and over.

[4] GED is General Educational Development high school equivalency diploma.

[5] Employment status is shown only for persons 18–64 years of age.

(*Source:* Family Core component of the 2007 National Health Interview Survey. The estimates for 2007 are based on data collected in January through June. Data are based on household interviews of a sample of the civilian non-institutionalized population.)

G   Interview three students using the questions you wrote.

H   In a small group, choose one of the three graphs or charts presented in this lesson. Recreate the graph or chart using information from the students in your class.

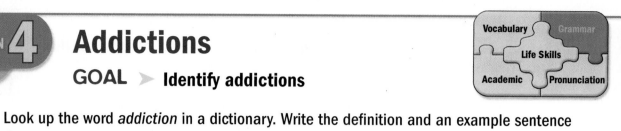

LESSON **4** **Addictions**

GOAL ➤ Identify addictions

A Look up the word *addiction* in a dictionary. Write the definition and an example sentence that uses the word.

addiction *n.* _____

_____

_____

B Work with a partner and brainstorm a list of addictions.

C Match the words below to their correct definitions and write the complete sentences on another piece of paper. Use a dictionary if you need to.

1. Tolerance is _____.

2. Impairment is _____.

3. Substance addiction is _____.

4. Physiological dependence is _____.

5. A twelve-step program is _____.

6. Psychological dependence is _____.

7. Process addiction is _____.

8. Detoxification is _____.

9. Withdrawal is _____.

10. An addict is _____.

a. the process of giving up a substance or activity to which a person has become addicted

b. a condition in which a person is dependent on some chemical substance, such as cocaine or heroin

c. a plan for overcoming an addiction by going through twelve stages of personal development

d. a condition in which a person requires certain activities or the intake of some substance in order to maintain mental stability

e. a condition in which a person is dependent on some type of behavior, such as gambling or shopping

f. an inability to carry on normal, everyday functions because of an addiction

g. the ability of the body to endure a certain amount of a substance

h. the process of adjusting to the absence of some substance or activity that a person has become addicted

i. a person physically or emotionally dependent on a substance or an activity

j. a condition in which a person's body requires certain behaviors or the intake of some substance, without which it will become physically ill

D Look at the list of addictions below. Which ones are substance (S) addictions and which ones are process (P) addictions? Circle your choice.

Addictions		
alcohol S P	food S P	shopping S P
caffeine S P	gambling S P	video games S P
prescription medicine S P	surfing the Internet S P	work S P
illegal drugs S P	smoking (nicotine) S P	

E In a small group, discuss the following questions.

1. Why do people become addicts?

2. What can you do if you are addicted to something?

3. What can you do to help a friend or family member who is addicted to something?

F Read the statements below. Do you think each person has an addiction problem? Circle *yes* or *no* and then give a reason for your answer.

1. Although my uncle Gerry sold his car to spend more time gaming in Las Vegas, he says he doesn't have a gambling problem.
   Addiction: yes no **Reason:** _____

2. Even though her sister spends thousands of dollars a month on her credit cards, she doesn't think she is a shopaholic.
   Addiction: yes no **Reason:** _____

3. Danielle is convinced she isn't addicted to caffeine although she has to drink two cups of coffee before she can get out of bed in the morning.
   Addiction: yes no **Reason:** _____

4. In spite of the fact that Fletcher plays video games for three hours a night instead of doing his homework, he denies he has a problem.
   Addiction: yes no **Reason:** _____

G   Study the chart with your classmates and teacher.

Adverb Clauses of Concession	
Dependent clause	**Independent clause**
Although he spends a lot of time in Las Vegas,	he says he doesn't have a gambling problem.
Even though her sister spends thousands of dollars a month,	she doesn't think she is a shopaholic.
Though she has to drink two cups of coffee before she can get out of bed in the morning,	she is convinced she isn't addicted to caffeine.
In spite of the fact that he plays video games for three hours a night,	he denies he has a problem.
Explanation: Adverb clauses of concession show a contrast in ideas. The main or independent clauses show the unexpected outcome. The unexpected outcome in the third example is that it is surprising that she thinks she isn't addicted to caffeine.	
Note: The clauses can be reversed and have the same meaning. Do not use a comma if the independent clause comes first in the sentence.	
Example: *She doesn't think she is a shopaholic even though she spends thousands of dollars a month.*	

H   Create sentences with dependent and independent clauses. Use the ideas below and the sentences in the chart as examples.

EXAMPLE: <u>Even though he smokes two packs of cigarettes a day, he doesn't think he</u>

<u>is addicted to nicotine.</u>

✓ nicotine addition/smokes two packs a day
Internet addiction/spends five hours a day online
shopping addiction/goes to the mall at least once a day
food addiction/weighs over 300 pounds
drug addiction/sold all his clothes to buy more drugs

1. _____

2. _____

3. _____

4. _____

I   Imagine a good friend of yours has an addiction to something. Write about his or her addiction. How is it affecting your friend's life? How is it affecting your life? How is your friendship different because of it?

First aid

GOAL ➤ **Interpret procedures for first aid**

A What does a first-aid kit have in it? Use the words in the box to label each item.

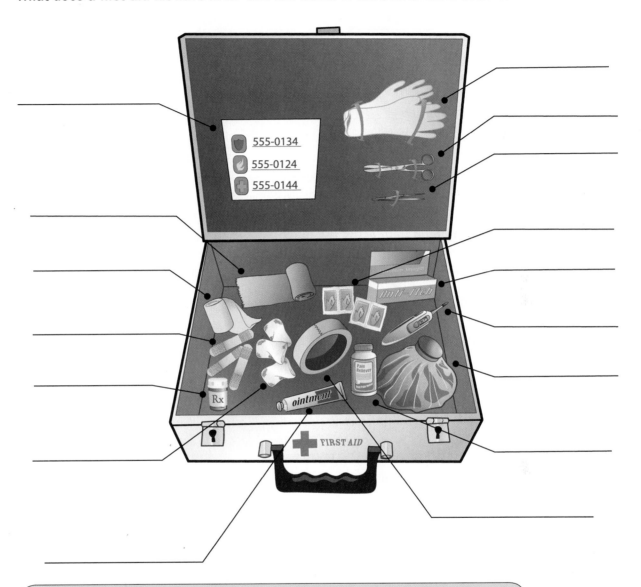

555-0134
555-0124
555-0144

Rx

ointment

FIRST AID

adhesive bandages	compress dressing	roller bandage
adhesive cloth tape	emergency phone numbers	scissors
antibiotic ointment	hydrocortisone ointment	sterile gauze pads
antiseptic wipes		sterile gloves
aspirin	prescription medication (optional)	thermometer
cold compress / ice pack		tweezers

B Do you have a first-aid kit at home or in your car? Why is each item important? Discuss your ideas with your classmates.

C   **Define the following injuries.**

1. burn: _____

2. choking: _____

3. poisoning: _____

4. open wound: _____

5. head injury: _____

6. shock: _____

D   **Look at the list of first-aid procedures below. Which injuries does each one apply to? Write the appropriate injuries on the line below each procedure.**

1. Call 911. _____ choking, poisoning, head injury, shock _____

2. Call Poison Control.

   _____

3. Control external bleeding.

   _____

4. Cover with a light gauze dressing.

   _____

5. Have the person lie down.

   _____

6. Help maintain body temperature.

   _____

7. Perform Heimlich maneuver.

   _____

8. Stop the bleeding with a piece of sterile gauze.

   _____

9. Strike the victim's back between the shoulder blades five times.

   _____

10. Treat wounds.

   _____

LESSON **5**   GOAL ➤ **Interpret procedures for first aid**

 E Read the chart below. Compare the information with your answers in Exercise D. Were you right?

First-Aid Procedures*		
Injury	**Do**	**Don't**
burn	Run cold water over burn area for 15 minutes. Cover the burn with a light gauze dressing. If blisters pop, apply a light antibiotic ointment and cover with light gauze dressing.	**Don't** put any creams or greases on the burned area. **Don't** pop any blisters. **Don't** use an ice pack.
choking	Call 911. Strike the victim's back between the shoulder blades five times. Perform Heimlich maneuver.	**Don't** give water to the person.
poisoning	Call 911 (if person is unconscious or having trouble breathing). Call Poison Control (800-222-1222).	**Don't** induce vomiting. **Don't** give the person anything to eat or drink.
open wound	Stop the bleeding with a piece of sterile gauze. Wash with soap and water (if minor), apply a thin layer of antibiotic ointment, and cover with a bandage.	**Don't** remove any object protruding from injury. **Don't** wash or apply ointment to a large, deep wound.
head injury	Call 911 if person is unconscious or drowsy. Treat wounds. Ice a small bump.	**Don't** leave the person alone, especially when sleeping. Instead, wake up every two to three hours and have the person answer simple questions.
shock	Call 911. Have the person lie down. Control external bleeding. Help maintain body temperature.	**Don't** raise the person's head. **Don't** give the person food or drink.

* Not all first-aid procedures for each injury are listed.

 F Divide the class into victims and good citizens. All "victims" should write one of the injuries from page 104 on an index card or piece of paper. Walk up to another student in the classroom and show him or her your card. Ask him or her what he or she would do. All "good citizens" should tell victims what you can do to help his or her injury.

EXAMPLE:
Victim: (Shows Good Citizen card that reads "Choking.")
Good Citizen says to Victim: "I'm going to call 911. Then, I'm going to strike your back five times between your shoulder blades. If that doesn't work, I'm going to perform the Heimlich maneuver. I will not give you water."

Review

A) Write one healthy solution for each problem. (Lesson 1)

1. Problem: eating fast food three times a week because no time to cook

   Solution: _____

2. Problem: high blood pressure and at risk for diabetes

   Solution: _____

3. Problem: really stressed at work

   Solution: _____

4. Problem: overweight children

   Solution: _____

B) Read the bill and write four questions you would ask the doctor's office about it. (Lesson 2)

PATIENT NAME: Reed, Jacob			PROVIDER NAME: Robert Wickern, M.D.	
Date	**Procedure**	**Description of Service**	**Co-Pay**	**Amount Payable**
8/23/2008	99391	Well-Child Check		$150.00
8/23/2008	90700	DTaP Vaccine		$30.00
8/23/2008	90465	Vaccine Admin		$44.00
8/23/2008	90645	Hib Vaccine		$32.00
8/23/2008	90466	Vaccine Admin		$64.00
8/23/2008		Patient Co-Pay	-$25.00	
9/17/2008		Primary Insurance Payment		-$200.00
9/17/2008		Uncollectible		-$75.00
		Amount Due		

1. _____

2. _____

3. _____

4. _____

C) Work with a partner and have a conversation between a patient and the doctor's office with the questions you wrote. Switch roles. (Lesson 2)

D Read the bar graph. Then, answer the questions below it. (Lesson 3)

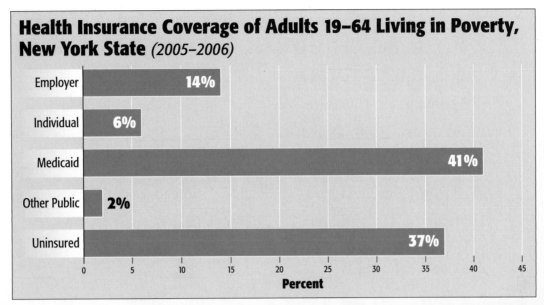

Health Insurance Coverage of Adults 19–64 Living in Poverty, New York State *(2005–2006)*

Employer — 14%
Individual — 6%
Medicaid — 41%
Other Public — 2%
Uninsured — 37%

Percent

(*Sources:* Urban Institute and Kaiser Commission on Medicaid and the Uninsured estimates based on the Census Bureau's March 2006 and 2007 Current Population Survey (CPS: Annual Social and Economic Supplements). Web site: http://www.statehealthfacts. org/comparebar.jsp?ind=131&cat=3)

1. What percentage of adults is uninsured? _____

2. What percentage of adults is insured by their employers? _____

3. What percentage of adults is on Medicaid? _____

4. What percentage of adults has insurance coverage? _____

E Write sentences on a separate piece of paper combining the ideas below. (Lesson 4)

EXAMPLE: nicotine addiction/smokes two packs of cigarettes a day
Even though he smokes two packs of cigarettes a day, he doesn't think he
is addicted to nicotine.

1. exercise addiction /works out 3 times a day   3. food addiction /eats all day long
2. sleeping addiction /sleeps 11 hours a night   4. coffee addiction /drinks 4 cups a day

F Write down six injuries you learned about in this unit. In a group, discuss the first-aid procedures for each injury in Exercise F. (Lesson 5)

_____   _____   _____

_____   _____   _____

VOCABULARY REVIEW

G Choose the correct word for each sentence.

1. _____ helps me relax when I've had a long day at work.

   a. Detoxification   b. Meditation   c. Tolerance   d. Depression

2. They think she has a sleeping-pill _____.

   a. process   b. insurance   c. depression   d. addiction

3. If you are with someone who is in _____, you should call 911.

   a. shock   b. out of shape   c. meditation   d. treatment

4. How would you _____ someone who has a head injury?

   a. affect   b. treat   c. impair   d. insure

5. Jared's body has built up a _____ to alcohol since he has been drinking for so long.

   a. tolerance   b. substance   c. detoxification   d. withdrawal

H Give two examples of each of the following items.

1. Substance addictions: _____ _____

2. Process addictions: _____ _____

3. First-aid kit items: _____ _____

4. Items on a medical bill: _____ _____

I Write original sentences for each of the following terms.

1. uninsured: _____

2. at risk: _____

3. self-esteem: _____

4. responsible party: _____

5. survive: _____

Research Project

A There are many health-related resources in every community. If you wanted to find the following local resources, what would you do?

1. gym: _____

2. eye doctor: _____

3. medical clinic: _____

B Using three different research methods, find the locations and contact information for the following community resources. Write down the name of one specific place you found with each research method.

Community resource	Internet	Phone book	Friends and/or Family
swimming pool Name: _____			
drug-and-alcohol rehabilitation center Name: _____			
health clinic Name: _____			
dentist Name: _____			
fire station Name: _____			
first aid/CPR course Name: _____			
ambulance service Name: _____			
health insurance Name: _____			

Team Project

Give a presentation on a health-related topic.

Presentation Topics

- Healthy Practices
- Medical Bills
- Health Insurance
- Addictions
- First Aid

1. Form a team with four or five students. Decide which topic your team will work on. (Each team should choose a different topic.)

2. Choose positions for each member of your team.

POSITION	JOB DESCRIPTION	STUDENT NAME
Student 1: **Project Leader**	See that everyone speaks English. See that everyone participates.	
Student 2: **Secretary**	Take notes on your team's ideas.	
Student 3: **Coordinator**	Divide presentation into parts. Assign each team member one part of presentation.	
Student 4: **Director**	Organize presentation so that individual parts create a unified whole.	
Student 5: **Members**	Do assigned part of presentation. Supportively critique other members' work as they rehearse their parts of presentation.	

3. Gather information for your presentation from this book and other sources.

4. Decide how to present your material creatively. For example, you can use charts, skits, or encourage class participation.

5. Create any materials needed for your presentation.

6. Practice your presentation.

7. Give your presentation to the class.

Retail

GOALS

➤ **Do product research**
➤ **Purchase goods and services by phone and Internet**
➤ **Interpret product guarantees and warranties**
➤ **Return a product**
➤ **Sell a product**

Vocabulary Builder

 A Using the words in the box below, discuss the picture with a partner. Look up the words you do not know in a dictionary.

EXAMPLE: *This woman is asking the salesperson about the product warranty.*

convince	exchange	free of charge	guarantee
make	model	policy	quality
receipt	refund	research	return
review	transaction	warranty	

Vocabulary Builder

B Look at the following goals in this unit. Then, look back at the words and phrases from Exercise A. Decide which words and phrases go with each goal. Write them on the lines after each goal. (Some words and phrases can be used with more than one goal.)

1. Do product research: _____

_____

2. Purchase goods and services by phone and Internet: _____

_____

3. Interpret product guarantees and warranties: _____

_____

4. Return a product: _____

_____

5. Sell a product: _____

_____

C Knowing a synonym for an unfamiliar word will often help you better understand its meaning. Find synonyms for the words below in a dictionary or thesaurus.

Word	Synonym
1. allege	
2. conform	
3. convince	
4. exchange	
5. fault	
6. guarantee	
7. malfunction	
8. model	
9. quality	
10. refund	
11. research	
12. return	
13. review	

How much is it?

GOAL ➤ Do product research

A Imagine that you are going to buy the following products. In a group, discuss what information you need to research before you make your purchases. Write your ideas on the line next to each item.

1. a bed: _____

2. a refrigerator: _____

3. a television: _____

4. a cell phone: _____

5. an air conditioner: _____

6. a car: _____

B Listen to the conversation Maya is having with the salesperson. What does she want to know about the patio set? Write her questions below. Some questions are embedded.

CD
TR 28

1. _____

2. _____

3. _____

4. _____

5. _____

6. _____

7. _____

8. _____

C How did the salesperson answer the questions above? Discuss these answers with your classmates.

D Look at the list of ways to research a product. Which methods have you used before?

- Ask friends and family
- Ask the salesperson
- Go online and read product reviews
- Read a consumer magazine

E Maya went online to research the patio furniture she saw in the store. Read the product reviews she found.

U-RATE-IT

http://U-Rate-It/patio_furniture

U-RATE-IT *Patio Furniture Reviews from Actual Buyers* ADD YOUR RATING

AcmeFurniture 4 REVIEWS

⭐⭐☆☆☆ *Good-Looking, But Poor Quality*
The cushions are almost flat after a few sittings. The fabric started pilling and I thought we could remove the fabric to wash it, but that's not the case. It stains easily. Not for outdoors or indoors. Not worth spending your money on.

⭐☆☆☆☆ *Not for Outdoors*
This set is NOT for outdoor use. We bought this set in June, and by the end of the summer it looked TERRIBLE. Our patio gets late afternoon sun, and after a month the wood stain started to fade. We are going to stain it with deck stain to try to make it last another year. But for the amount we paid, we are very disappointed in the quality.

⭐⭐⭐⭐⭐ *Love It!*
I bought this set in May and absolutely LOVE it! It is under a gazebo and gets wet from the rain, but I haven't had any splitting or mold that the other people are talking about. If it rains, you just have to put the seat cushions up so they can dry...simple. It's comfortable and I would buy it again! Maybe some other people got a "bad batch" or something. Love it!

⭐⭐⭐☆☆ *You Get What You Pay For*
I purchased this beautiful set for our open-air, roofless patio about three weeks ago. So far, it has endured California weather. The wood is too thin to endure year-round exposure. Even the owner's manual suggests covering it when not in use. Our plan is to enjoy it now and stash it away in the garage after summer. This set was on sale at the time we made the purchase, and I'm glad I didn't pay full price. If you want longevity and to worry less about your wood furniture, spend a little more for the heavier woods. I would give 5 stars for the "look," and 2 ¾ stars for "quality." If we had paid full price for this set, it would have made its way back to the store.

F Based on the reviews, would you buy this patio furniture if it were on sale? Why or why not? Which review made the biggest impression on you? Why?

_____

_____

_____

G Think of something you have bought recently. Write a review for it on a separate piece of paper.

H   Imagine that you are buying a new refrigerator. What questions would you ask before you made your decision to purchase a particular model? Write some ideas below.

1. _____

2. _____

3. _____

I   Think about the refrigerator in your home. Answer the following questions. (If you don't know the answer, make it up.)

1. What is the make and model? _____

2. How much did it cost? _____

3. Where did you buy it? _____

4. How is the quality? _____

5. Have you ever had any problems with it? _____

6. Did it come with a warranty? _____

7. What do you like about it? _____

8. What do you not like about it? _____

J   In order to research different refrigerator models, talk to your classmates. Ask them the questions you wrote in Exercise H as well the ones in Exercise I.

K   Based on your product research, what kind of refrigerator would you buy?

_____

L   Choose one of the items from Exercise A to purchase. Do product research by reading reviews on the Internet or talking to your classmates. What did you find out about this product? Write some of the things you learned below.

_____

_____

_____

Shopping from home

GOAL ➤ Purchase goods and services by phone and Internet

Vocabulary • Grammar • Life Skills • Academic • Pronunciation

A Take a class poll. How many of your classmates shop online? How many of your classmates order from catalogs?

B Look at the page from a housewares catalog. Find each of the following pieces of information for each product: item name, item description, item price, and item number.

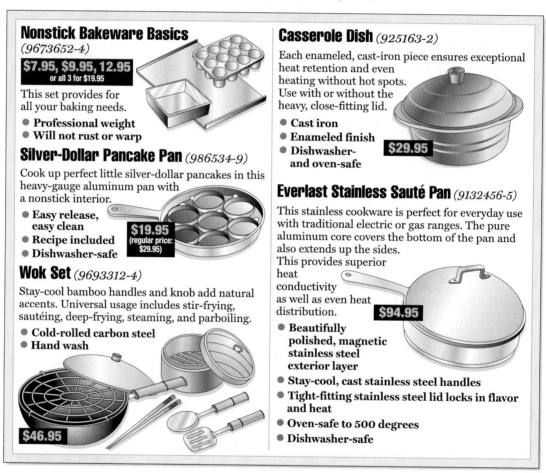

Nonstick Bakeware Basics (9673652-4)

$7.95, $9.95, 12.95 or all 3 for $19.95

This set provides for all your baking needs.
- Professional weight
- Will not rust or warp

Silver-Dollar Pancake Pan (986534-9)

Cook up perfect little silver-dollar pancakes in this heavy-gauge aluminum pan with a nonstick interior.
- Easy release, easy clean
- Recipe included
- Dishwasher-safe

$19.95 (regular price: $29.95)

Wok Set (9693312-4)

Stay-cool bamboo handles and knob add natural accents. Universal usage includes stir-frying, sautéing, deep-frying, steaming, and parboiling.
- Cold-rolled carbon steel
- Hand wash

$46.95

Casserole Dish (925163-2)

Each enameled, cast-iron piece ensures exceptional heat retention and even heating without hot spots. Use with or without the heavy, close-fitting lid.
- Cast iron
- Enameled finish
- Dishwasher- and oven-safe

$29.95

Everlast Stainless Sauté Pan (9132456-5)

This stainless cookware is perfect for everyday use with traditional electric or gas ranges. The pure aluminum core covers the bottom of the pan and also extends up the sides. This provides superior heat conductivity as well as even heat distribution.
- Beautifully polished, magnetic stainless steel exterior layer
- Stay-cool, cast stainless steel handles
- Tight-fitting stainless steel lid locks in flavor and heat
- Oven-safe to 500 degrees
- Dishwasher-safe

$94.95

CD TR 29

C Listen to four phone conversations between salespeople and customers who are buying items from this catalog page. Complete the chart below based on what you hear.

	Item	Total cost	Method of payment
1.			
2.			
3.			
4.			

LESSON 2

GOAL ➤ **Purchase goods and services by phone and Internet**

D With your teacher, review the process of making a purchase online. Look for each step in the screen shots below.

1. Find the Web site you want to buy something from.
2. Perform a search.
3. Look at the results of your search.
4. Narrow down the results to one item.
5. Make purchase.

E In a group, discuss the pros and cons of buying something online. Make two lists on a separate piece of paper.

GOAL ➤ **Purchase goods and services by phone and Internet**

F What kinds of things are good to buy on the Internet? _____

_____

G With a partner, create a list of specific items that could be sold in a catalog or online.

1. Decide what type of items you could sell.
2. On a separate piece of paper, create art, descriptions, and prices for at least five items.

H Exchange your page with another pair of students. Have a conversation about purchasing the new items with your partner. One of you should be a sales representative explaining your products. Sit back-to-back to simulate selling and purchasing on the phone.

I Do an Internet search to find items similar to the ones on the catalog page in Exercise B. Follow the steps in Exercise D to find the items you want.

If you don't have computer access, answer the following questions.

1. What would you like to buy online? _____

2. What words will you type in to search for that item? _____

3. Do you know of an online store that sells this item? _____

4. Once you click on the store that sells your item, what information will you look for?

_____

_____

5. How will you decide if you are going to purchase the item? What information will you consider?

_____

_____

Is this under warranty?

GOAL ➤ Interpret product guarantees and warranties

Vocabulary | Grammar
Life Skills
Academic | Pronunciation

A Think about the following situations and make some decisions with a partner.

What would you do if . . .

1. the air-conditioning in your car wasn't cold enough?

2. your printer stopped working one week after you bought it?

3. the speaker on your cell phone didn't work?

4. you washed a new shirt according to the care instructions on the tag and it shrank?

B A *warranty* or *guarantee* is a written promise by a company to replace or repair a product free of charge within a certain time period after purchase if it has any defects. Read the following warranty for home-stereo speakers.

> This product is guaranteed against all defects in workmanship and materials for two years following purchase. All it takes to ensure complete coverage is to register your purchase. Once you have warranty-registered your product, the nearest service center can respond rapidly and directly to you.

C Answer the following questions about the warranty.

1. Where do you take your product if something goes wrong?

_____

2. How long is the product guaranteed?

_____

3. What do you need to do to make sure you receive the warranty for the product?

_____

4. Does the warranty cover your dropping and breaking the product?

_____

GOAL ➤ Interpret product guarantees
and warranties

D Warranties are often worded with legal language that can be difficult to understand. Look at the example below and see how it can be restated more clearly.

> Seller warrants to the original customers purchasing products from Seller that all such products, under normal use and operation, will be free from defects in materials and workmanship affecting form, fit, and function.

In other words . . .

The seller says that if I use this product under normal conditions, as it was meant

to be used, there won't be any problems with it.

E Restate each sentence below in your own words.

1. Any claims alleging failure of products to conform to the foregoing warranty may be made only by the customer who purchased the product.

   _____

   _____

2. The foregoing warranty only applies while the product is being used in the original machine with the original hardware and software configuration.

   _____

   _____

3. Seller, at its option, will repair, replace, or provide a credit or refund of either the original purchase price less a restock fee or current fair market value, whichever is less, for any product Seller deems to be defective.

   _____

   _____

4. The above warranties cover only defects arising under normal use and do not include malfunctions or failures from misuse, neglect, alteration, abuse, improper installation, or acts of nature.

   _____

   _____

5. Removal of the labeling on products will void all warranties.

   _____

   _____

F Read the following guarantee from a printer company.

OUR NO-HASSLE GUARANTEE

Our products are backed the way they are built—the best in the industry. Our no-hassle printer guarantee gives you excellent product support with no worries, no hassles. Now you can enjoy the benefit of a substitute printer if your printer fails during the first 30 days of use.

We will send a replacement printer to you within 48 hours of your request for any printer that fails to meet the factory specifications or fails to power up upon delivery within 30 days of your invoice date. No hassles. Upon receipt of your no-hassle replacement printer, you must return your defective printer to us. Your defective printer will be exchanged for the same make and model, or for a printer of equal value. In addition, if your printer has three separate quality issues, which are documented with our technical support team, within one year from the date of your invoice, we will permanently replace your defective printer with a new printer of equal or greater value.

G Choose the best answer.

1. You can receive a substitute printer if your printer doesn't work during the first
   a. 48 hours.   b. 30 days.   c. week.

2. How soon will you receive your substitute printer?
   a. 48 hours   b. 30 days   c. one week

3. When you receive your replacement printer, you must
   a. return the defective printer.   b. do nothing.   c. call the company.

4. If you have three problems with your printer during the first year, the company will
   a. fix your printer for free.   b. refund your money.   c. permanently replace the printer.

H With a partner, choose a product from the list below and write your own guarantee. Use the ideas from the three warranties you have read in this lesson, but use your own words.

digital camera   bicycle   cell phone   washing machine

 LESSON 4 **Returns and exchanges**

GOAL ➤ Return a product

A Think of some things you have returned to the stores where you bought them. What did you return and why? Discuss your experiences with your classmates.

 B Read and listen to the conversation.

CD
TR 30

Sales Associate: Can I help you with something?
Customer: Yes, I'd like to return these shoes. I wore them around my house on the carpet for a few days and they are still uncomfortable. The salesman who sold them to me insisted they would stretch out and soften up, but they haven't. I'd like to get my money back.
Sales Associate: I'm afraid I can't give you your money back. These were on sale and we don't offer refunds for sale items.
Customer: Can I exchange them?
Sales Associate: Yes, you can exchange them for something of equal value.
Customer: OK, I'll do that. Let me look around for a bit.
Sales Associate: Take your time.

  C Listen to each question and write the correct answer.

CD
TR 31

1. _____

2. _____

3. _____

4. _____

5. _____

6. _____

D Read each return policy and the statements below it. Circle *T* (true) or *F* (false).

> Thank you for shopping at Nico's. Return or exchange for merchandise within 2 weeks with tags attached and/or in original packaging. Original sales receipt is required for full refund. Final sale on all sale items.

1. You can exchange sale items.   T   F
2. You need an original sales receipt for a refund.   T   F

> Valid photo ID required for all returns (except for credit card purchases), exchanges, and to receive and redeem store credit. With a receipt, a full refund in the original form of payment, except payments made with checks, will be issued for new and unread books and unopened music within 4 days. For merchandise purchased with a check, a store credit will be issued within the first 7 days. Without an original receipt, a store credit issued by mail will be offered at the lowest selling price. With a receipt, returns of new and unread books and unopened music from our Web site can be made for store credit. Textbooks after 14 days or without a receipt are not returnable. Used books are not returnable.

3. If you pay with a check, you can get cash back.   T   F
4. You cannot return used books.   T   F
5. If you have a receipt, you can get a refund on unopened
   music within four days.   T   F
6. If you don't have a receipt, you can exchange an item.   T   F

> All returns and exchanges must be new, unused, and have original packaging and accessories. Some items cannot be returned if opened. For our full return and exchange policy, visit the store or log onto our Web site. For a gift receipt, bring this receipt back to any store within 90 days. Ask about receipt look-up.

7. All opened items can be exchanged.   T   F

> We will not be undersold. Guaranteed! If you find a lower price at any of our competitors, we will meet that price.

8. This store will offer you a lower price than its competitors. T   F

E Look back at all the false statements. (*Hint:* There are five.) On a separate piece of paper, rewrite each statement, making it true.

CD
TR 32

F   Listen to six conversations and write the corresponding conversation number in front of the reason each person gave for returning the product. Then write what product the person returned.

Conversation #	Reason for returning or exchanging item	Was item returned or exchanged?
	bought the wrong package	
	already have them	
	bad reception	
	don't fit right	
	broken	
	doesn't work with computer	

G   Write two reasons you might return each of the items listed below.

1. digital video camera

    a. _____   b. _____

2. gallon of milk

    a. _____   b. _____

3. pair of pants

    a. _____   b. _____

4. laptop computer

    a. _____   b. _____

5. sunglasses

    a. _____   b. _____

6. textbook

    a. _____   b. _____

H   Divide the class into two halves—clerks and customers.

Clerks should help each customer with his or her return.

Customers should choose one item from Exercise G to return or exchange. Use one of the reasons you came up with. Have at least three conversations with different clerks or customers and then switch roles.

For sale!

GOAL ➤ **Sell a product**

A If you were not going to go out physically to buy something in an actual store, where would you shop? Brainstorm ideas with a partner.

B If you were going to sell some items you owned, what would they be? Make a list on a separate piece of paper.

C Read each of the ads below and think about the following questions.

1. What is for sale?
2. How is the seller trying to convince you to buy it?
3. Would you consider buying any of the items in the ads? Why or why not?

This car, a sporty red convertible, will make you feel like royalty. **Rare Red Dino 1973 Ferrari 246 GTS.** Right-hand drive, 50,000 miles before restoration, 10,500 miles after. One owner. Serious inquiries only. (784) 555-9712

Looking for a great place to sit? Watch movies? Chat with friends? This brown leather couch, a part of our family for years, will be the most comfortable piece of furniture you have ever sat on. Come sit on it today. $890. (732) 555-3337

I bought too many tickets for the Taylor Band. These tickets, the best seats in the house, are selling for face value. I have a total of eight available tickets but will sell them separately. From $60. E-mail me at tix@redhouse.com

Save on gas! Buy a bicycle! This bike, a fun means of transportation, will get you around in style. In great shape and only six months old. Take it for a test ride. $275. spin@buyitcheap.com

D Read about appositives with your classmates and teacher.

Appositives		
Noun or Noun Phrase	**Appositive**	**Remainder of sentence (Predicate)**
The ad,	**the one with all the great pictures,**	makes me want to buy those dishes.
That computer,	**the fastest machine in the store,**	sells for over $2,000.

Explanation:
• An appositive is a noun or noun phrase that renames another noun next to it in a sentence.
• The appositive adds extra descriptive detail, explains, or identifies something about the noun.
• An appositive can come before or after the noun phrase it is modifying.

Example: *A helpful gift, money is always appreciated by a newly married couple.*

Note: Appositives are usually set off by commas.

E Find and underline the appositives in the ads on the previous page. There is one appositive in each ad.

F Complete each of the statements below with an appositive.

EXAMPLE: Her dress, _____a really fancy gown_____, got the attention of every customer in the room.

1. That used car, _____, will probably be for sale for quite a while.

2. Used pots and pans, _____, are hard to sell without the matching lids.

3. Two round-trip plane tickets, _____, can be used to travel anywhere in the United States.

4. The MP3 player, _____, can hold over 2,000 songs.

5. Those leather shoes, _____, have many more years of walking in them.

6. This restaurant, _____, will make you money as soon as you open the doors.

7. That set of suitcases, _____, will carry enough clothing and accessories for two weeks of traveling.

8. Her Web site, _____, is an online store with tons of gently worn clothes for sale.

G If you wanted to buy the following things (not in a store), where would you look?

1. car: _____

2. shoes: _____

3. CDs (music): _____

4. furniture: _____

H Imagine that you are going to sell something. Answer the questions below.

1. What would you sell? _____

2. What would you say to make your product sound appealing?

_____

3. How much would you sell it for? _____

4. Where would you place your ad? _____

5. How would you want people to contact you? _____

I Write three statements with appositives that you would use in your advertisement.

1. _____

2. _____

3. _____

J On another piece of paper, write an ad to sell your product. Find an attractive photo or create a drawing to draw attention to your ad.

K Share your ad with your classmates. See if you can find anyone who would buy what you are selling.

Review

A Imagine that you are going to buy a used car. Write four questions you would ask car owners who want to sell their car. (Lesson 1)

1. _____
2. _____
3. _____
4. _____

B Ask your classmates the questions you wrote in Exercise A. Write some of their responses below. When your classmates ask you their questions, you can talk about your own car or a car you are familiar with. (Lesson 1)

_____

_____

_____

C Imagine that you are going to buy a product online. Write a short paragraph about the steps you will need to take to buy the product. (Lesson 2)

First, I will go online. _____

_____

_____

_____

_____

D Look back at the sample catalog on page 116. With a partner, practice buying and selling three of the items listed on the page. (Lesson 2)

E Write a conversation about one of the items on page 116. Continue on another piece of paper if needed. (Lesson 2)

Salesperson: _____

Customer: _____

Salesperson: _____

Customer: _____

Salesperson: _____

Customer: _____

F Read the following warranty and circle *T* (true) or *F* (false). (Lesson 3)

> CLARICO warrants this product against defects in material and workmanship under normal use and service for one year from the original purchase date. CLARICO will repair or replace the defective product covered by this warranty. Please retain the dated sales receipt as evidence of the date of purchase. You will need it for any warranty service. In order to keep this warranty in effect, the product must have been handled and used as described in the instructions accompanying this warranty. This warranty does not cover any damage due to accident, misuse, abuse, or negligence.

1. This warranty is good for two years.   T   F
2. CLARICO will replace your product if it gets stolen.   T   F
3. You need your receipt to get service under this warranty.   T   F
4. This warranty covers product defects.   T   F

G Working in pairs, practice asking questions about returning items. One student is a customer and one is a clerk. Switch roles. Use the following return policy to explain the rules. (Lesson 4)

> Valid photo ID required for all returns (except for credit card purchases), exchanges, and to receive and redeem store credit. With a receipt, a full refund in the original form of payment, except payments made with checks, will be issued for new and unread books and unopened music within 4 days. For merchandise purchased with a check, a store credit will be issued within the first 7 days. Without an original receipt, a store credit issued by mail will be offered at the lowest selling price. With a receipt, returns of new and unread books and unopened music from our Web site can be made for store credit. Textbooks after 14 days or without a receipt are not returnable. Used books are not returnable.

1. return books with the original receipt
2. return textbooks after three weeks

3. return two calendars without a receipt
4. exchange CDs that have not been opened

H Write appositives to complete each statement below. (Lesson 5)

1. This pre-owned car, _____, has been thoroughly inspected and is in tip-top shape.

2. This laptop computer, _____, still has a two-year warranty.

3. Two theater tickets, _____, can be used any weeknight in the month of August.

4. The bicycle, _____, has barely been ridden.

I Using one of the statements in Exercise H, write an ad for the product on another piece of paper. Include an appositive somewhere in the ad. (Lesson 5)

VOCABULARY REVIEW

J Use the following words in a sentence.

1. allege: _____

2. guarantee: _____

3. quality: _____

4. convince: _____

5. malfunction: _____

6. policy: _____

K Share your sentences with a partner. Write your partner's best sentence below.

_____

L Match each word to its synonym.

Word

1. return _____

2. refund _____

3. model _____

4. guarantee _____

5. exchange _____

6. convince _____

7. conform _____

8. allege _____

Synonym

a. claim

b. promise

c. match

d. replace

e. reimburse

f. persuade

g. type

h. take back

Research Project

A There are quite a few ways to sell things. What items might you try to sell using the following methods?

1. Placing an ad in the newspaper: _____

2. Having a yard sale: _____

3. Posting a sign on the sale item: _____

_____

4. Placing an ad at a local community center, church, or library: _____

_____

5. Listing the item on an online auction site: _____

B Can you think of other ways to sell something? Write down your ideas.

_____

_____

C Imagine that you are going to sell something. Find out what is involved in using the two methods below. Write notes after each method. (*Ideas:* How much does it cost to place the ad? How long will the ad stay up? How many words can you write?)

Placing an ad in the newspaper: _____

_____

_____

_____

_____

_____

Listing an item on an online auction site: _____

_____

_____

_____

_____

_____

Team Project

Create an online or catalog-only store.

1. Form a team with four or five students. Choose positions for each member of your team.

POSITION	JOB DESCRIPTION	STUDENT NAME
Student 1: **Project Leader**	See that everyone speaks English. See that everyone participates.	
Student 2: **Secretary**	Take notes on your team's ideas.	
Student 3: **Designer**	Design layout of catalog or Web page.	
Student 4: **Director**	Assign each team member one part of presentation. Organize presentation so that individual parts create a unified whole.	
Student 5: **Assistant**	Help secretary and designer with their work.	

2. Decide the name of your store and what you will sell. Select a variety of items to sell.

3. Create the following items for your store: catalog or Web pages, the store's return policy, and a warranty/guarantee policy.

4. Prepare a poster that contains all of the information in Steps 2 and 3.

5. Present your store's catalog pages or Web pages to the class.

The Office

GOALS

➤ Identify and use technology
➤ Resolve technology problems
➤ Establish an organizational system

➤ Identify and resolve problems at work
➤ Report progress

Vocabulary Builder

Vocabulary | Grammar
Life Skills
Academic | Pronunciation

A Use the terms in the box below to label each item you might find in an office. Under each item, write a brief description of its purpose.

business telephone	fax machine	LCD projector	photocopier
~~laptop computer~~	flash drive	paper shredder	printer
external hard drive	label maker	PDA	scanner

laptop computer: process

information, create reports

and do Internet research

_____   _____   _____

_____   _____   _____

_____   _____   _____

_____   _____   _____   _____

_____   _____   _____   _____

_____   _____   _____   _____

Vocabulary Builder

_____   _____   _____   _____

_____   _____   _____   _____

_____

B A great way to remember vocabulary is to draw a picture of the items you are learning. Look up the following words if you don't know them and draw a picture for each one. (Remember to look for the definition that is related to technology.)

handset	cable	port	memory card

C These three technology terms cannot be easily drawn. Write a definition for each one.

1. troubleshoot: _____

2. paper jam: _____

3. feed: _____

D Look at the verbs in the chart below. Find the nouns and adjectives in the verbs' word families. (*Hint:* Not every verb has an adjective in its family.)

Verb	Noun	Adjective
compete		
collaborate		
avoid		
accommodate		
compromise		
motivate		
resolve		

How do you turn it on?

GOAL ➤ **Identify and use technology**

A Read the instructions for connecting a printer.

Instructions for Connecting Your Printer

1. Take the **printer** out of the box and set it next to your **computer**.

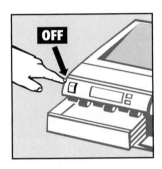

2. Make sure the printer is **off**.

3. Plug the **power supply cord** into the back of the printer and then plug it into the wall socket.

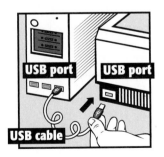

4. Plug one end of the **USB cable** into the **USB port** on the back of the printer. Plug the other end into the **USB port** on the computer.

B Reread the instructions until you completely understand them. Then, in your own words, tell a partner how to connect a printer to a computer. (If you have a computer and printer in your classroom, you can explain the steps as you do them.)

(**C**) Connecting an external hard drive is similar to connecting a printer. Match each of the instructions below to the correct picture. Then, label each computer part in the diagrams below with the bold words from the instructions.

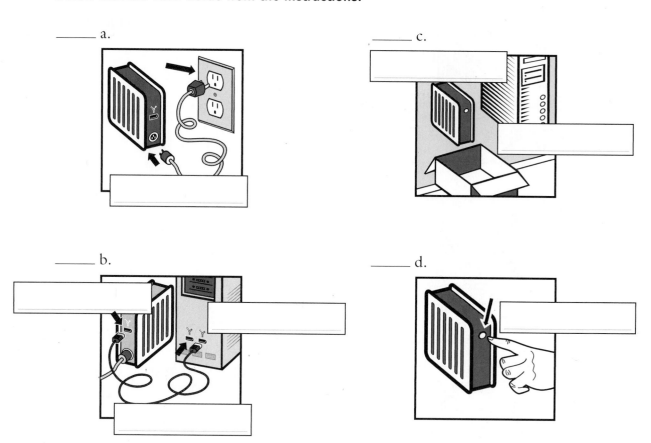

_____ a.

_____ b.

_____ c.

_____ d.

1. Take the **external hard drive** out of the box and set it next to your **computer**.

2. Make sure the external hard drive is **off**.

3. Plug the **external power supply** into the back of the external hard drive and then plug it into the wall socket.

4. Plug one end of the **firewire cable** into the **firewire port** on the back of the external hard drive. Plug the other end into the **firewire port** on the computer.

LESSON 1 **GOAL** ➤ **Identify and use technology**

D Read the excerpt from a fax machine manual and answer the questions that follow it.

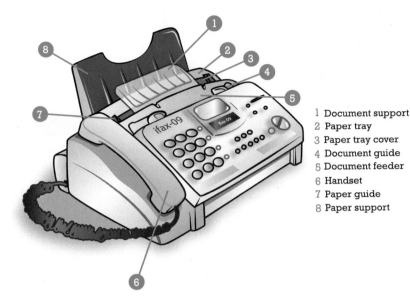

1 Document support
2 Paper tray
3 Paper tray cover
4 Document guide
5 Document feeder
6 Handset
7 Paper guide
8 Paper support

QUICK START

This chapter gives you a brief introduction to the basic functions of the fax machine. Please refer to the rest of the manual for more detailed instructions.

SENDING A FAX

1. Place the document to be sent (up to 15 pages) in the document feeder.

2. Dial the number in one of the following ways:

a. Dial the number and press start.

b. Lift the handset, dial the number, and press start.

c. Push the speakerphone button, dial the number, and press start.

d. Press and hold the one-touch button. *(See one-touch dialing on page 15.)*

e. Press the speed-dial button, enter a speed-dial code, and press start. *(See speed dialing on page 16.)*

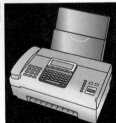

RECEIVING A FAX

There are three modes for receiving faxes:

1. FAX mode: The fax machine will answer the phone, detect fax tones, and receive the fax.

2. AUTO answer mode: The telephone rings for a certain number of rings and then switches to fax receiving.

3. TEL answer mode:
You must manually receive the fax:

a. Answer the phone.

b. If you hear a fax tone, press the start button.

c. Once you hear the fax tones from both machines, hang up the phone to receive the fax.

1. When sending a fax, how many different ways are there to dial? _____

2. Which method doesn't require pushing the start button? _____

3. How many pages can you fax at once? _____

4. How many ways are there to receive a fax? _____

5. Which mode requires that you answer the phone? _____

E Look back at the list of technology items on pages 133–134. Choose one item that you are familiar with and write a list of instructions with illustrations. Review instructions with a partner for clarity.

How do you fix it?

GOAL ➤ **Resolve technology problems**

Vocabulary Grammar
Life Skills
Academic Pronunciation

A Think of some problems you have had in the past with technology. What were the problems? How did you fix them? In a small group, discuss your problems.

B Carla is having trouble with her fax machine. For some reason, no paper comes out when she tries to receive a fax. Read what she found in her manual under *troubleshooting*.

Problem	Solution
Paper jams during printing.	Remove the jammed paper by pulling it out smoothly. If the paper tears while you are removing it, make sure that no small pieces are left inside the machine.
Paper sticks together.	Make sure you don't have more than 40 sheets in the paper tray. Take the paper out, fan the pages, and put them back in. (Humidity can cause pages to stick together.)
Paper won't feed.	Remove any obstructions from inside the printer.
Multiple sheets of paper feed at the same time.	When loading the paper, do not force the paper down into the printer. If multiple sheets have caused a paper jam, clear it.

C Answer the questions based on the troubleshooting guide.

1. What should you do if paper tears while you are removing it from the printer?

_____

2. How many sheets can the paper tray hold? _____

3. What causes pages to stick together? _____

4. What should you do if the paper won't feed? _____

_____

5. What should you do if there is a paper jam? _____

_____

D Based on the information above, what are three suggestions you might give Carla?

1._____

2._____

3._____

LESSON 2 **GOAL** ➤ **Resolve technology problems**

CD
TR 33

E Listen to the conversations between employees at a small printing company. Write the problems and suggestions for fixing them in the chart below.

Problem	Suggestions
	1. 2.
	1.
	1. 2. 3.

F Maya has to take pictures for her job as a home appraiser. She is having some problems with her digital camera. Look at her manual below and match each problem to its possible solution.

Problem

1. Camera will not operate. _____
2. Camera won't take any more pictures or video. _____
3. Only a few pictures will fit on the memory card. _____
4. Battery loses its charge quickly. _____
5. Pictures won't display on the LCD screen. _____

Solution

a. Turn LCD screen on.
b. Turn camera on.

c. Replace battery.

d. Clear memory card.
e. Take pictures at a lower resolution.

G Read the troubleshooting guide for the label maker. Fill in the best answer for each question and statement on the next page.

Problem	Solution
1. The display stays blank after you have turned on the machine.	Check that the AC adaptor is connected correctly. If you are using batteries, check that they are inserted correctly. If the batteries are low, replace them.
2. The machine doesn't print or the printed characters are blurred.	Check that the tape cassette has been inserted properly. If the tape cassette is empty, replace it. Make sure the tape compartment cover has been closed.
3. The text files that you stored in the memory are no longer there.	Replace the batteries.
4. A blank horizontal line appears through the printed label.	Clean the printhead.
5. Striped tape appears.	You have reached the end of the tape. Replace the tape cassette with a new one.

GOAL ➤ **Resolve technology problems**

1. You should clean the printhead when
   - ○ a. striped tape appears.
   - ○ b. a horizontal line appears.
   - ○ c. the display is blank.

2. When your files from memory are no longer there, you should
   - ○ a. connect the AC adaptor.
   - ○ b. clean the printhead.
   - ○ c. replace the batteries.

3. What can you do if the printed characters are blurred?
   - ○ a. Replace the tape cassette.
   - ○ b. Replace the batteries.
   - ○ c. Clean the printhead.

4. What does striped tape mean?
   - ○ a. The printhead is dirty.
   - ○ b. The tape cassette needs to be replaced.
   - ○ c. The tape compartment needs to be closed.

H In a small group, ask for help with the technology problems below. Write down their suggestions in the chart below.

Problem	Suggestions
My fax machine won't send a fax.	
There is no dial tone on my telephone.	
My printer won't print.	
My paper shredder won't shred.	
The copier keeps jamming.	

I Share the suggestions you received with your other classmates. Which suggestions are the best?

Files and folders

GOAL ➤ **Establish an organizational system**

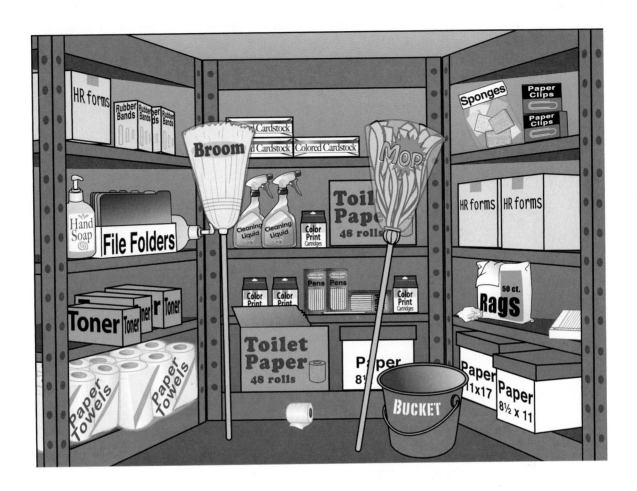

A One way of organizing things is by putting similar items in groups. How would you organize this supply closet? Discuss your solutions with your classmates.

B On a separate piece of paper, reorganize the supply closet. Do a simple drawing of the closet with shelves and cabinets and show where you would keep each item.

GOAL ➤ Establish an organizational system

Vocabulary · Grammar · Life Skills · Academic · Pronunciation

C Each file folder below represents a place to file certain documents. Take the list of documents below the folders and write the letter of the document in the folder where it fits.

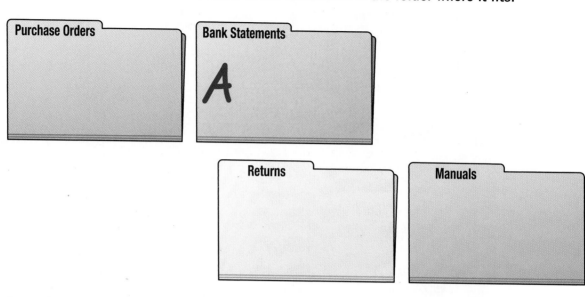

Purchase Orders	Bank Statements
	A

Returns   Manuals

A. Bank of the East Statement for March
B. Canyon i867 User Guide
C. City National Bank Statement for April
D. Claire's Order #7654
E. Delpi Photo Plus Manual
F. Dresses 'n' More Order #7625

G. Fancy Pants Return #7986
H. HL Printer 5000 User Guide
I. Jimbo's Return #7893
J. Leapin' Lizards Return #5678
K. Pink Lady Order #6879
L. Sunshine Girls Order #9864

D One way of organizing things is by putting them in alphabetical order. Rewrite the list of folders from above in alphabetical order.

1. _____   3. _____

2. _____   4. _____

E Organize the purchase orders and returns in Exercise C in numerical order. List them in order below.

Purchase Orders

1. _____

2. _____

3. _____

4. _____

Returns

1. _____

2. _____

3. _____

F   Lars knows he needs to get organized in his home office. Read about his problem and solution.

Problem: My financial papers are very disorganized. They are in huge piles on my desk and in piles in my desk drawers.

Solution: I'm going to buy hanging files and file folders. The tabs on my hanging files will be labeled as follows: Bank Accounts, Credit Cards, Income, Investments, Retirement Accounts, Liabilities, Insurance, Real Estate, and Tax Returns. Each hanging folder will be a different color and inside there will be file folders of that same color. For example, in my Bank Account file there will be a file folder for each of the three banks where I have accounts. Inside those folders, I will keep my bank statements and any papers related to that account.

G   In a small group, come up with organizing solutions for these problems.

1. **Problem:** There are over 300 books scattered about the office, in bookshelves, on people's desks, and on the floor next to desks.

   Solution: _____

   _____

2. **Problem:** Supply closet has supplies everywhere; nothing can be found.

   Solution: _____

   _____

3. **Problem:** Papers are very disorganized; there are stacks of papers everywhere.

   Solution: _____

   _____

H   Think of an organizational problem you have at home, perhaps in your refrigerator, pantry, or garage. Describe the problem below and write out a detailed solution.

_____

_____

_____

_____

_____

What's the problem?

GOAL ➤ Identify and resolve problems at work

 A Answer the following questions with a partner.

1. What is *conflict resolution*?
2. Where are some places that conflicts might occur?
3. Who are some people that you might have conflicts with?
4. Think about the ways you handle conflicts with people. What would you say your personal style of behavior is when speaking to people in conflict?

B As you read the article on the next few pages, think about the following questions. When you have finished, come back and answer them.

1. What are the three benefits to resolving conflict?
2. What can happen if conflict is not handled effectively?
3. What are the five different conflict styles in Thomas and Kilmann's theory?
4. What does *IBR* stand for? What are the six steps of the IBR approach?
5. What are the five steps for resolving conflict?

Conflict Resolution: Resolving Conflict Rationally and Effectively

In many cases, conflict in the workplace just seems to be a fact of life. We've all seen situations where different people with different goals and needs have come into conflict. And we've all seen the often intense personal animosity that can result.

The fact that conflict exists, however, is not necessarily a bad thing: As long as it is resolved effectively, it can lead to personal and professional growth.

The good news is that by resolving conflict successfully, you can solve many of the problems that it has brought to the surface, as well as getting benefits that you might not at first expect:

1. **Increased understanding**: The discussion needed to resolve conflict expands people's awareness of the situation, giving them an insight into how they can achieve their own goals without undermining those of other people;

2. **Increased group cohesion**: When conflict is resolved effectively, team members can develop stronger mutual respect and a renewed faith in their ability to work together;

3. **Improved self-knowledge:** Conflict pushes individuals to examine their goals in close detail, helping them understand the things that are most important to them, sharpening their focus, and enhancing their effectiveness.

However, if conflict is not handled effectively, the results can be damaging. Conflicting goals can quickly turn into personal dislike. Teamwork breaks down. Talent is wasted as people disengage from their work. And it's easy to end up in a vicious downward spiral of negativity and recrimination. If you're to keep your team or organization working effectively, you need to stop this downward spiral as soon as you can. To do this, it helps to understand two of the theories that lie behind effective conflict-resolution techniques.

Understanding the Theory: *Conflict Styles*

In the 1970s, Kenneth Thomas and Ralph Kilmann identified five main styles of dealing with conflict that vary in their degrees of cooperativeness and assertiveness.

Competitive: People who tend towards a competitive style take a firm stand and know what they want. They usually operate from a position of power, drawn from things like title, rank, expertise, or persuasive ability. This style can be useful when there is an emergency and a decision needs to be made fast; when the decision is unpopular; or when defending against someone who is trying to exploit the situation selfishly. However, it can leave people feeling bruised, unsatisfied, and resentful when used in less urgent situations.

(Continued)

Collaborative: People tending towards a collaborative style try to meet the needs of all people involved. These people can be highly assertive but, unlike the competitor, they cooperate effectively and acknowledge that everyone is important. This style is useful when you need to bring together a variety of viewpoints to get the best solution; when there have been previous conflicts in the group; or when the situation is too important for a simple trade-off.

Compromising: People who prefer a compromising style try to find a solution that will at least partially satisfy everyone. Everyone is expected to give up something, and the compromiser also expects to relinquish something. Compromise is useful when the cost of conflict is higher than the cost of losing ground, when equal strength opponents are at a standstill, and when there is a deadline looming.

Accommodating: This style indicates a willingness to meet the needs of others at the expense of the person's own needs. The accommodator often knows when to give in to others, but can be persuaded to surrender a position even when it is not warranted. This person is not assertive but is highly cooperative. Accommodation is appropriate when the issues matter more to the other party, when peace is more valuable than winning, or when you want to be in a position to collect on this "favor" you gave. However, people may not return favors, and overall this approach is unlikely to give the best outcomes.

Avoiding: People tending towards this style seek to evade the conflict entirely. This style is typified by delegating controversial decisions, accepting default decisions, and not wanting to hurt anyone's feelings. It can be appropriate when victory is impossible, when the controversy is trivial, or when someone else is in a better position to solve the problem. However, in many situations this is a weak and ineffective approach to take.

Understanding the Theory: *The Interest-based Relational Approach*

Once you understand the different styles, you can use them to think about the most appropriate approach (or mixture of approaches) for the situation you're in. You can also think about your own instinctive approach and learn how you need to change this if necessary.

The second theory is commonly referred to as the Interest-Based Relational (IBR) Approach. This conflict-resolution strategy respects individual differences while helping people avoid becoming too entrenched in a fixed position. In resolving conflict using this approach, you follow these rules:

1. **Make sure that good relationships are the first priority.** As far as possible, make sure that you treat the other calmly and that you try to build mutual respect. Do your best to be courteous to one-another and remain constructive under pressure.
2. **Keep people and problems separate.** Recognize that in many cases the other person is not just "being difficult"—real and valid differences can lie behind conflictive positions. By separating the problem from the person, real issues can be debated without damaging working relationships.
3. **Pay attention to the interests that are being presented.** By listening carefully you'll most likely understand why the person is adopting his or her position.
4. **Listen first; talk second.** To solve a problem effectively, you have to understand *where the other person is coming from* before defending your own position.
5. **Set out the "facts."** Agree and establish the objective, observable elements that will have an impact on the decision.
6. **Explore options together.** Be open to the idea that a third position may exist, and that you can get to this idea jointly.

By following these rules, you can often keep contentious discussions positive and constructive. This helps to prevent the antagonism and dislike which so often causes conflict to spin out of control.

Using the Tool: *A Conflict-Resolution Process*

Based on these approaches, a starting point for dealing with conflict is to identify the overriding conflict style employed by yourself, your team, or your organization. Look at the circumstances and think about the style that may be appropriate. Then use the process below to resolve the conflict.

(Continued)

Step One: Set the scene.

Make sure that people understand that the conflict may be a mutual problem, which may be best resolved through discussion and negotiation rather than through raw aggression. If you are involved in the conflict, emphasize the fact that you are presenting your perception of the problem. Use active listening skills to ensure you hear and understand others' positions and perceptions. And make sure that when you talk, you're using an adult, assertive approach rather than a submissive or aggressive style.

Step Two: Gather information.

Here you are trying to get to the underlying interests, needs, and concerns of the other people involved. Ask for the other people's viewpoints and confirm that you respect their opinions and need their cooperation to solve the problem. Try to understand their motivations and goals and see how your actions may be affecting them.

Step Three: Agree on the problem.

This sounds like an obvious step, but often different underlying needs, interests, and goals can cause people to perceive problems very differently. You'll need to agree on the problems that you are trying to solve before you'll find a mutually acceptable solution. Sometimes different people will see different but interlocking problems—if you can't reach a common perception of the problem, then, at the very least, you need to understand what the other people see as the problem.

Step Four: Brainstorm possible solutions.

If everyone is going to feel satisfied with the resolution, it will help if everyone has had fair input in generating solutions. Brainstorm possible solutions and be open to all ideas, including ones you never considered before.

Step Five: Negotiate a solution.

By this stage, the conflict may be resolved—both sides may better understand the position of the other, and a mutually satisfactory solution may be clear to all.

There are three guiding principles here: *Be Calm, Be Patient, Have Respect.* Managed in the wrong way, real and legitimate differences between people can quickly spiral out of control, resulting in situations where cooperation breaks down and the team's mission is threatened. This is particularly the case when the wrong approaches to conflict resolution are used.

To calm these situations down, it helps to take a positive approach to conflict resolution, where discussion is courteous and nonconfrontational, and the focus is on issues rather than on individuals. If this is done, then, as long as people listen carefully and explore facts, issues, and possible solutions properly, conflict can often be resolved effectively.

(Source: Used with permission from ©Mind Tools Ltd, 1995–2008, All rights reserved.)

C On another piece of paper, make a list of all the vocabulary words in the article that are unfamiliar to you. Choose ten that are the most important to your understanding of the article. Define them and write example sentences.

D Choose one of the following topics and write a one-paragraph summary.

1. Thomas and Killman's five conflict styles
2. The IBR approach
3. The five steps of the conflict-resolution process

LESSON 5

What did you do?

GOAL ➤ Report progress

A Maria's supervisor has asked her to write a progress report about a long-term project she is working on. Read the guidelines he gave her.

Progress Report Guidelines

You write a progress report to inform a supervisor, associate, or customer about progress you've made on a project over a certain period of time. In the progress report, you explain any or all of the following:

- how much of the work is complete,
- what part of the work is currently in progress,
- what work remains to be done,
- what problems or unexpected things, if any, have arisen,
- how the project is going in general.

(Source: Reprinted with permission from David A. McMurrey, author of *Power Tools for Technical Communication*, Boston: Heinle. 2001.)

B Read part of Maria's report. Is she following the guidelines so far?

To: Henry Kim, Human Resources Director
From: Maria Avalos
Date: April 14, 2008
Subject: Program for Employee Training

It seems that many problems have arisen from the employees working such long hours and not being able to communicate effectively with one another. It was proposed that I put together a training program for our employees on conflict resolution.

So far, I have been conducting research on whether it is better to bring in an outside training organization or do the training ourselves. I have concluded that it would be more cost-effective for us to do the training ourselves. So, I am currently working on putting together a training manual that can be used for the conflict-resolution training. I foresee that it will take me another two weeks to complete the manual. Once it has been completed, we will need to choose several people to conduct the training and train them to be effective leaders.

C What does Maria still need to include in her report?

1. _____

2. _____

D Study the chart with your classmates and teacher.

Noun Clauses as Objects		
Subject + Verb	**Noun clause**	**Explanation**
I did	*what* I was asked.	• A noun clause starts with a question word or *that* and is followed by a subject and verb. • In these examples, the noun clauses are the objects of the sentences.
She knows	*how* the computer works.	
They decided	*where* the location would be.	
My boss asked	*who* would be best for the job.	
I hope	*that* they work as a team.	

E Complete each of the sentences below with an appropriate noun clause from the list. More than one noun clause may be appropriate.

> how the filing system worked   where the files were
> ~~what she told me to~~   who got to receive the training
> that they would be promoted   how to complete the progress report
> that we knew what we were doing   who wanted to be the team leader

1. I did <u>what she told me to</u>_____.

2. She found _____.

3. The supervisor asked _____.

4. He explained _____.

5. Our team showed _____.

6. Sari asked _____.

7. Jared and Giulia hoped _____.

8. The representative chose _____.

F Complete each sentence with a noun clause of your own.

1. I asked _____.

2. I hoped _____.

3. I decided _____.

4. I explained _____.

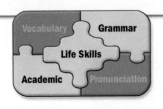

 Maria reports that she has encountered a few more problems in addition to those she mentioned in her report in Exercise B.

- The employees do not want this training.
- None of the supervisors who could be trainers want to lead the training.

Write a paragraph from Maria's perspective. Add the problems mentioned above to her report. Include what she might suggest as solutions.

_____

_____

_____

_____

_____

_____

_____

_____

 Write a progress report using the guidelines from page 147. Use the format of Maria's report. Use the information below for your report.

Project: Organize the files for the entire company

Work completed: Half of the stacks of papers in all the offices have been organized

Doing now: Currently organizing the other half of the stacks

To do: Still need to create labels for hanging files and file folders

Problems: Employees don't want me to come into their offices

Progress: Good

Using the examples in Exercises D and E, include a few noun clauses in your report.

Review

 A Read the instructions for setting up an MP3 player and answer the questions that follow. (Lesson 1)

> ### Setting Up Your MP3 Player
>
> Step 1: Charge the battery.
> Step 2: Install the software.
> Step 3: Import music to your computer.
> Step 4: Connect the MP3 player to your computer and transfer music.
> Step 5: Play music.

1. What do you need to do before you import music to your computer?

   _____

2. What can you do after you have transferred music?

   _____

3. What is the first thing you must do?

   _____

4. What must you do in order to be able to transfer music?

   _____

 B Read the tips and troubleshooting advice for the MP3 player. Then, choose the best answer. (Lesson 2)

> Most problems can be resolved by resetting your MP3 player.
>   To reset your MP3 player:
>
>   1. Connect it to a power outlet using the power adaptor.
>   2. Toggle the hold switch on and off.
>   3. Press and hold the menu button for at least 10 seconds.
>
> If your player won't turn on or respond:
>
>   • Make sure the hold switch is off.
>   • If you're using the remote, make sure the remote's hold switch is off.
>   • Recharge your battery.

1. How can you solve most problems with your MP3 player?
   a. Recharge the battery.   b. Turn it on and off.   c. Reset it.

2. What button do you hold down when resetting the player?
   a. Hold   b. Menu   c. Power Adaptor

3. What's the first thing you should do to reset your player?
   a. Make sure the hold switch is off.
   b. Connect it to a power outlet.
   c. Hold down the menu button.

C Alphabetize the following items. (Lesson 3)

paper shredder	business telephone	scanner
flash drive	label maker	external hard drive
LCD projector	computer	printer
cables	fax machine	power adaptors

D How would you organize these items in an office? Write a brief explanation.

_____

_____

_____

_____

E Answer the following questions about the conflict-resolution article. (Lesson 4)

1. What are the three benefits to resolving conflict?

a. _____

b. _____

c. _____

2. What are the five different conflict styles in Thomas and Kilmann's theory?

a. _____ d. _____

b. _____ e. _____

c. _____

3. What are the six steps of the IBR approach?

a. _____ d. _____

b. _____ e. _____

c. _____ f. _____

4. What are the five steps for resolving conflict?

a. _____ d. _____

b. _____ e. _____

c. _____

F Name the five things a progress report should include. (Lesson 5)

VOCABULARY REVIEW

 G Put each word below in the correct column according to its part of speech: *noun*, *verb*, or *adjective*.

cost-effective	reorganize	organize	hanging files	fan
feed	effective	splotchy	paper jam	long-term
obstructions	force	faded	toner	power supply

Noun	Verb	Adjective
1. _____	1. _____	1. _____
2. _____	2. _____	2. _____
3. _____	3. _____	3. _____
4. _____	4. _____	4. _____
5. _____	5. _____	5. _____

H Use words from Exercise G to complete the sentences. Not all the words are used.

1. Did you get a chance to put the _____ in alphabetical order?

2. The computer wasn't working because the _____ wasn't plugged in.

3. If you _____ out the paper, it shouldn't stick together so much.

4. It doesn't seem _____ to have so many computers running at the same time. That wastes a lot of energy.

5. Tim, can you _____ these files? They seem to have gotten out of order.

6. If you _____ the paper into the feeder, it will probably cause a

   _____.

7. When I opened up the fax machine, I couldn't see any_____.

8. We need a/an _____ solution to this disorganized supply closet.

9. Is there any more _____ in the supply closet? These copies are

   _____ and _____.

10. I wonder why the paper won't _____ through the printer correctly?

Research Project

A In the past two units, you have learned about two different areas of work: the retail setting and the office. In a group, brainstorm a list of jobs that might be found in each of these areas.

Retail jobs	Office jobs

B Look back at your two lists. Circle the jobs that you think earn the most money.

C Using the Internet or printed materials from your teacher, research jobs and see if you can add any more to your lists above.

D Now choose two or three jobs that seem the most interesting to you and find out the following information.

Job title	Salary	Training/Qualifications required	Related occupations

Team Project

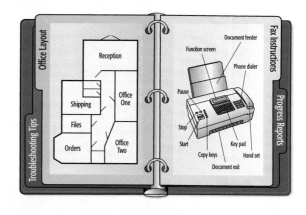

Set up a typical business office.

1. Form a team with four or five students. Choose positions for each member of your team.

POSITION	JOB DESCRIPTION	STUDENT NAME
Student 1: **Project Leader**	See that everyone speaks English. See that everyone participates.	
Student 2: **Secretary**	Take notes on your team's ideas.	
Student 3: **Designer**	Design layout of the office.	
Student 4: **Tech Writer**	Write up instructions for use and troubleshooting tips for two pieces of technology in the office.	
Student 5: **Documenter**	Write a progress report about the process.	

2. Decide what kind of office your team will create (what you do, how many employees you have, etc.).

3. Make an alphabetized inventory list of all the items in your office and how many of each item your office has.

4. Draw a diagram of your office and indicate where everything is located.

5. Choose two pieces of technology in your office and write up instructions for use as well as troubleshooting tips.

6. Write a progress report explaining what you did. Include any conflicts you may have had with team members while completing the project.

7. As a team, present your office documents to the class. Be prepared to explain why you set up the office the way you did.

Civic Responsibility

GOALS

➤ Identify requirements for establishing residency and citizenship
➤ Understand your rights
➤ Identify local civic organizations
➤ Interpret information about environmental issues
➤ Communicate your opinion

Vocabulary Builder

A Guessing the meaning of a word from the context of its sentence is called *making an inference*. Read each sentence and guess the meaning of the italicized word and its part of speech. Then, look it up in a dictionary to check if you got it right.

1. The judge gave an *impartial* verdict that did not favor either side.

   Part of speech: _____ Meaning: _____

   Dictionary definition: _____

2. There are so many *commuters* on the roads today that there is always a lot of pollution and noise.

   Part of speech: _____ Meaning: _____

   Dictionary definition: _____

3. We all must *conserve* energy so our kids don't have to worry when they get older.

   Part of speech: _____ Meaning: _____

   Dictionary definition: _____

4. During the war, many *refugees* went to safer countries to try to live better lives.

   Part of speech: _____ Meaning: _____

   Dictionary definition: _____

5. She runs a *charitable* organization that gives food to homeless people.

   Part of speech: _____ Meaning: _____

   Dictionary definition: _____

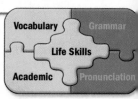

B Each sentence in Exercise A reflects the topic of a lesson in this unit. Look at each sentence and guess what you think the lesson will be about. (*Hint:* Look at the goals listed at the top of page 155.)

1. _____

2. _____

3. _____

4. _____

5. _____

C Look at the list of terms below and categorize each word or phrase by writing it under the correct lesson title.

alien	conserve	punishment	reusable
bear arms	eligible	refugee	slavery
believe	naturalization	peaceably assemble	social welfare
capital crime	opinion	resource	status
civic	protect		

Identify requirements for establishing residency and citizenship	Identify your rights	Identify local civic organizations	Interpret information about environmental issues	Communicate your opinion

D Write your own sentence for each of the words below.

1. naturalization: _____

2. punishment: _____

3. civic: _____

4. reusable: _____

5. resource: _____

Investigating citizenship

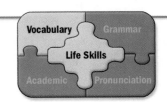

GOAL ➤ **Identify requirements for establishing residency and citizenship**

Ⓐ How can an immigrant become a permanent resident of the United States? Make a list of your ideas below.

1. _____
2. _____
3. _____
4. _____

Ⓑ Several students in Mrs. Morgan's class want to become permanent residents of the United States. Read about each nonresident below and decide if you think he or she is eligible to become a permanent resident. Write *yes* or *no*.

1. Hanh has been living in the U.S. since 1985. She recently became engaged to a U.S. citizen. Is she eligible? _____

2. Sadiq is a refugee from Iraq who has been here for six months. Is he eligible? _____

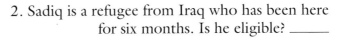

3. Ella is 35 and her mother just became a permanent resident. Is she eligible? _____

4. Phillipe has lived in the U.S. since 1965. Is he eligible? _____

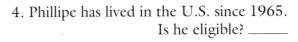

5. Enrique's wife just became a permanent resident. Is he eligible? _____

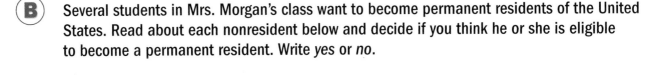

C Read the following information found on the Web site of U.S. Citizenship and Immigration Services (www.uscis.gov).

You may be *eligible* to apply for adjustment to permanent resident status if you are already in the United States *and* if one or more of the following categories apply to you.

Family Member 1. You are the spouse, parent, unmarried child under age 21, the unmarried son or daughter over age 21, the married son or daughter, or the brother or sister of a United States citizen and have a visa petition approved in your behalf. 2. You are the spouse or unmarried son or daughter of any age of a lawful permanent resident and you have a family-based visa petition approved in your behalf.

Employment You are an alien who has an approved visa petition filed in your behalf by a United States employer.

Fiancé You were a fiancé who was admitted to the United States on a K-1 visa and then married the U.S. citizen *who applied for the K-1 visa for you.* Your unmarried, minor children are also eligible for adjustment of status. If you did not marry the U.S. citizen who filed the K-1 petition in your behalf, or if you married another U.S. citizen or lawful permanent resident, you are not eligible to adjust status in the United States.

Asylee You are an asylee or refugee who has been in the United States for at least a year after being given asylum or refugee status and still qualify for asylum or refugee status.

Diversity Visa You received notice from the Department of State that you have won a visa in the Diversity Visa Lottery.

U.S. Resident Since Before 01/01/72 You have been a continuous resident of the United States since before January 1, 1972.

Parent's Lawful Permanent Resident (LPR) Status Your parent became a lawful permanent resident after you were born. You may be eligible to receive following-to-join benefits if you are the unmarried child under age 21 of the lawful permanent resident. In these cases, you may apply to adjust to permanent resident status at the same time that your parent applies for following-to-join benefits for you.

Spouse's LPR Status Your spouse became a lawful permanent resident after you were married. You may be eligible to receive following-to-join benefits. In these cases, you may apply to adjust to permanent resident status at the same time that your spouse applies for following-to-join benefits for you.

D Look back at each of the nonresidents in Exercise B. Do you need to change some of your answers? Discuss each situation with a partner and decide what specific details would make each person eligible for permanent resident status.

CD
TR 34

E Listen to the immigration officer talk about how to become a citizen. Fill in the missing words.

United States (U.S.) citizenship carries many _____ with it. The decision to become a U.S. citizen is a very important one. Being granted U.S. citizenship is known as _____. In most cases, a person who wants to naturalize must first be a _____ resident. By becoming a U.S. citizen, you gain many _____ that permanent residents or others do not have, including the _____. To be eligible for naturalization, you must first meet certain _____ set by U.S. law.

What are the basic requirements to apply for naturalization?
Generally, to be eligible for naturalization you must:
• Be age _____ or older; and
• Be a permanent resident for a certain amount of time (usually 5 years); and
• Be a person of good _____ character; and
• Have a basic knowledge of U.S. _____ and government; and
• Have a period of _____ residence and physical presence in the U.S.; and
• Be able to read, _____, and speak basic English. There are exceptions to this rule for someone who:
  – Is _____ years old and has been a permanent resident for at least 15 years; or
  – Is _____ years old and has been a permanent resident for at least 20 years; or
  – Has a physical or mental impairment that makes them unable to _____ these requirements.

When can I apply for naturalization?
You may be able to apply for naturalization if you are at least 18 years of age and have been a permanent resident of the U.S.:
• For at least _____ years; or
• For at least _____ years during which time you have been, and continue to be, married to and living in marriage with your U.S. citizen husband or wife; or
• Have honorable service in the U.S. military. Certain _____ of U.S. citizens and members of the military may be able to file for naturalization sooner than noted above previously.

(*Source:* www.uscis.gov)

F Discuss these questions with a partner: How many requirements are there to apply for naturalization? What are they?

G Think about people you know who have become permanent residents or citizens. Write short paragraphs about them following the example below.

My cousin has been living in the U.S. for ten years. Two years ago, her employer filed a visa petition for her to become a permanent resident, so she could stay and work for the company. The petition was approved and she got her green card last year.

Rights

GOAL ➤ **Understand your rights**

> *"A bill of rights is what the people are entitled to against every government on earth, general or particular, and what no just government should refuse, or rest on inference."*
>
> —Thomas Jefferson

A What do you think this quotation means?

B In 1791 the Bill of Rights was added to the United States Constitution. It is composed of the Constitution's first ten amendments. Read the Bill of Rights below. In a small group, paraphrase each amendment.

Amendment I Congress shall make no law respecting an establishment of religion, or prohibiting the free exercise thereof; or abridging the freedom of speech, or of the press; or the right of the people peaceably to assemble, and to petition the government for a redress of grievances.

Amendment II A well regulated militia, being necessary to the security of a free state, the right of the people to keep and bear arms, shall not be infringed.

Amendment III No soldier shall, in time of peace be quartered in any house, without the consent of the owner, nor in time of war, but in a manner to be prescribed by law.

Amendment IV The right of the people to be secure in their persons, houses, papers, and effects, against unreasonable searches and seizures, shall not be violated, and no warrants shall issue, but upon probable cause, supported by oath or affirmation, and particularly describing the place to be searched, and the persons or things to be seized.

Amendment V No person shall be held to answer for a capital, or otherwise infamous crime, unless on a presentment or indictment of a grand jury, except in cases arising in the land or naval forces, or in the militia, when in actual service in time of war or public danger; nor shall any person be subject for the same offense to be twice put in jeopardy of life or limb; nor shall be compelled in any criminal case to be a witness against himself, nor be deprived of life, liberty, or property, without due process of law; nor shall private property be taken for public use, without just compensation.

Amendment VI In all criminal prosecutions, the accused shall enjoy the right to a speedy and public trial, by an impartial jury of the state and district wherein the crime shall have been committed, which district shall have been previously ascertained by law, and to be informed of the nature and cause of the accusation; to be confronted with the witnesses against him; to have compulsory process for obtaining witnesses in his favor, and to have the assistance of counsel for his defense.

Amendment VII In suits at common law, where the value in controversy shall exceed twenty dollars, the right of trial by jury shall be preserved, and no fact tried by a jury, shall be otherwise reexamined in any court of the United States, than according to the rules of the common law.

Amendment VIII Excessive bail shall not be required, nor excessive fines imposed, nor cruel and unusual punishments inflicted.

Amendment IX The enumeration in the Constitution, of certain rights, shall not be construed to deny or disparage others retained by the people.

Amendment X The powers not delegated to the United States by the Constitution, nor prohibited by it to the states, are reserved to the states respectively, or to the people.

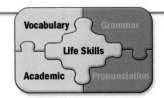
C Match each amendment with the right it guarantees.

1. The first amendment guarantees _____.

2. The second amendment guarantees _____.

3. The third amendment guarantees _____.

4. The fourth amendment guarantees _____.

5. The fifth amendment guarantees _____.

6. The sixth amendment guarantees _____.

7. The seventh amendment guarantees _____.

8. The eighth amendment guarantees _____.

9. The ninth amendment guarantees _____.

10. The tenth amendment guarantees _____.

a. a speedy and public trial by an impartial jury

b. the right to be charged by a grand jury if accused of a serious crime

c. people have other rights not listed in the Bill of Rights

d. freedom of religion

e. people, homes, and belongings are protected from unreasonable search and seizure

f. right to keep and bear arms

g. people have all the rights not given to the government by the Constitution

h. that government cannot force people to house soldiers during times of peace

i. a trial by jury in civil cases (dispute between private parties or between the government and a private party)

j. no excessive bail or fines will be imposed and that punishment will not be cruel and unusual

D Read each situation. Then, decide which amendment describes your rights. Write the amendment number on the line.

1. Your friend is Christian and celebrates Easter, but you are Jewish. _____

2. You have a registered gun in your house, locked up in a safe. _____

3. The police can't come into your home without a warrant. _____

4. If you are convicted of a crime, your punishment will not be cruel. _____

5. If you are accused of a crime, you will get a fair trial. _____

E There are currently 27 amendments to the Constitution. Read some of these other important amendments and answer the questions that follow.

> **Amendment XIII (1865)**
> Neither slavery nor involuntary servitude, except as a punishment for crime whereof the party shall have been duly convicted, shall exist within the United States, or any place subject to their jurisdiction.
>
> **Amendment XV (1870)**
> The right of citizens of the United States to vote shall not be denied or abridged by the United States or by any state on account of race, color, or previous condition of servitude.
>
> **Amendment XIX (1920)**
> The right of citizens of the United States to vote shall not be denied or abridged by the United States or by any state on account of sex.
>
> **Amendment XXVI (1971)**
> The right of citizens of the United States, who are 18 years of age or older, to vote, shall not be denied or abridged by the United States or any state on account of age.

1. What does the thirteenth amendment guarantee? _____

2. The fifteenth, nineteenth, and twenty-sixth amendments are all about the same right. What is it? _____

3. What is the difference between these three amendments?

   _____

   _____

4. In the original Constitution, why do you think so many groups of people were not given the right to vote? _____

   _____

F Discuss the following questions with a small group.

Do any of the rights identified in this lesson affect your life? Which ones? In what ways?

G Create a Bill of Rights for your classroom or school.

Getting involved

GOAL ➤ **Identify local civic organizations**

 A Read about the Mothers' Club of Northville, Michigan.

The Mothers' Club is a group of 35 dynamic women working to help Northville school children excel by providing enrichment materials and opportunities.

History

In 1935, a group of 12 women decided to meet regularly for enlightenment and social activities. During the Depression of the 1930's, the Mothers' Club held a fundraiser to purchase milk for school children to drink with their lunches. The Club's fundraising has now grown to three events each year, enabling the Club to donate approximately $30,000 annually to student enrichment programs and activities.

Fundraising

A. Fall: Mothers' Club hosts a booth during Northville's Victorian Festival.

B. Winter: *All Aglow* is an opportunity to honor or remember someone by purchasing a light on the community Christmas tree, located in front of the bandshell in downtown Northville.

C. Spring: *Hands to the Future*, a dinner and auction held annually in March, alternates every other year with … *The Community Telephone Directory*, distributed biannually to every household in the Northville School District

Community Service

Mothers' Club performs service projects at the public school buildings on a rotating cycle, working at two or three schools each year.

Social

1. Book club
2. Lunch and movie afternoons
3. Evening socials
4. Weekend getaways

(*Source:* Reprinted by permission of the City of Northville, MI. Web site: http://www.ci.northville.mi.us)

This club is an example of a *civic organization*. A civic organization is a group of people who come together for educational or charitable purposes, including the promotion of community welfare. The money generated by these clubs is devoted exclusively to charitable, educational, recreational, or social welfare purposes.

B Answer the following questions with a partner. Share your answers with others in your class.

1. What makes the Mothers' Club a civic organization?

_____

2. Can you think of any civic organizations in your community?

_____

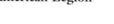

C   **Read about these civic organizations and answer the questions on the next page.**

American Legion

Purpose: To provide care for veterans and their families at hospitals and homes in the community
Members: Relatives of veterans
Annual Dues: $12

Boy Scouts

Purpose: To promote self-confidence, service to others, citizenship, and outdoor skills
Members: Boys only, at least 11 years old
Volunteer Scoutmasters: Male and female scoutmasters needed
Annual Dues: $25

Friends of the Library

Hiking Club

Purpose: To promote and support the local public library
Members: All welcome
Annual Dues: $15

Purpose: To enjoy the forest and also help raise public awareness of issues that face the present-day forest
Members: Anyone who enjoys hiking
Annual Dues: $10

Garden Club

Rotary Club

Purpose: To share experiences in gardening
Members: Anyone who enjoys gardening
Annual Dues: $15
Special Events: Plant sale

Purpose: To provide humanitarian service, encourage high ethical standards in all vocations, and help build goodwill and peace in the world
Members: To become a Rotarian, you must be invited to join a Rotary Club by a member of that club. A qualified candidate for Rotary-Club membership is an adult of good character and good business, professional, or community reputation.
Annual Dues: Amounts vary

1. Which clubs would you join if you liked nature? _____

2. Which clubs can you join if you are a woman? _____

_____

3. Which club has the highest dues? _____

The lowest? _____

4. Which clubs provide community service? _____

_____

5. If you could join one club, which one would it be? _____

Why? _____

D   **Some of the students from Mrs. Morgan's class want to create a civic organization. They have come together because they have common interests. Read about the students below and then come up with an idea for an organization.**

Hanh, Sadiq, Ella, Phillipe, and Enrique have just found out that many students at their school can't afford to buy books. There are over 100 students a year who attend class without textbooks. Hanh, Sadiq, Ella, Phillipe, and Enrique have one thing in common—they are all very creative. Sadiq takes beautiful photographs. Hanh and Ella both knit; they can make anything from hats to sweaters and blankets. Phillipe is an accomplished musician and songwriter, and Enrique paints oil paintings of flowers and animals.

Name of civic organization: _____

Purpose: _____

Members: _____

Annual dues: _____

Special events: _____

E   **Follow the directions for creating a civic organization.**

Step 1. Get together with a few students from your class and create a new civic organization. Complete the information about your organization below.

- Name of civic organization
- Purpose
- Members
- Annual dues
- Special events

Step 2. Now recruit members for your organization. You need at least ten members to be a true organization.

Saving the environment

GOAL ➤ Interpret information about environmental issues

 A Look at the list of ways to create less trash. Which ones do you do? Put a check (✔) next to them.

Create Less Trash

☐ Buy items in bulk from loose bins when possible to reduce the packaging wasted.
☐ Avoid products with several layers of packaging when only one is sufficient.
☐ Buy products that you can reuse.
☐ Maintain and repair durable products instead of buying new ones.
☐ Check reports for products that are easily repaired and have low breakdown rates.
☐ Reuse items like bags and containers when possible.
☐ Use cloth napkins instead of paper ones.
☐ Use reusable plates and utensils instead of disposable ones.
☐ Use reusable containers to store food instead of aluminum foil and cling wrap.
☐ Shop with a canvas bag instead of using paper and plastic bags.
☐ Buy rechargeable batteries for devices used frequently.
☐ Reuse packaging cartons and shipping materials. Old newspapers make
   great packaging material.
☐ Buy used furniture—there is a surplus of it, and it is much cheaper than new furniture.

(*Source:* Used with permission from Sustainable Environment for Quality of Life, www.seql.org)

B Interview your partner to find out how he or she conserves energy at home. Put a check (✔) next to the ones he or she does.

In Your Home—Conserve Energy

☐ Clean or replace air filters on your air-conditioning unit at least once a month.
☐ Lower the thermostat on your water heater to 120°F.
☐ Wrap your water heater in an insulated blanket.
☐ Turn down or shut off your water heater when you will be away for extended periods.
☐ Turn off unneeded lights even when leaving a room for a short time.
☐ Set your refrigerator temperature at 36 to 38°F and your freezer at 0 to 5°F.
☐ When using an oven, minimize door opening while it is in use.
☐ Clean the lint filter in your dryer after every load so that it uses less energy.
☐ Unplug seldom-used appliances.
☐ Use a microwave whenever you can instead of a conventional oven or stove.
☐ Wash clothes with warm or cold water instead of hot.
☐ Turn off lights, computers, and other appliances when not in use.
☐ Use compact fluorescent lightbulbs to save money and energy.
☐ Keep your thermostat at 68°F in winter and 78°F in summer.
☐ Use cold water instead of warm or hot water when possible.
☐ Connect your outdoor lights to a timer.

(*Source:* Used with permission from Sustainable Environment for Quality of Life, www.seql.org)

 C Sustainable Environment for Quality of Life (SEQL) has put together several action items that they would like to see accomplished in their communities in North and South Carolina. Read their plan for carpooling.

Carpooling: What is it?

Vanpooling/carpooling is an arrangement by a group of commuters to ride together from home or a prearranged meeting place in a van or a car to their destinations in a single round trip, with the driver as a fellow commuter. Vanpools/carpools usually consist of individuals who live near each other and are employees of the same company, or are employees of different companies located only a short distance apart, and have the same work hours. The great advantage of vanpools and carpools is that it reduces vehicle trips, reduces vehicle miles traveled, and therefore reduces auto emissions that result in poor air quality.

Shared Impact and Benefits
- Car- and vanpooling reduce overall auto emissions by reducing vehicle miles traveled, and by doing so, improve air quality. Ground-level ozone formation is reduced through the reduced levels of oxides of nitrogen from auto exhaust.
- The American Lung Association reports that low levels of ground-level ozone adversely affect nearly one-third of our population. So improvements in air quality result in improvements in public health.
- Peak-hour traffic congestion (and resulting gasoline consumption) are reduced. Nine billion gallons of fuel are wasted in traffic congestion each year—800 times the amount of oil spilled by the ship Exxon Valdez in 1989.
- Employers will be able to offer employees a value-added benefit and take a tax write-off.
- Eight of ten U.S. workers believe commuter benefits are valuable to employees.
- Furthermore, employers that pay for employee parking costs can save money.
- Vanpool/carpool participants save money by sharing commuting costs.

- Vanpool/carpool riders have lower stress commutes to work. Employers will also have more productive employees with higher morale.

Costs
Usually vanpoolers/carpoolers will share the costs of gasoline, maintenance, and/or leasing the vehicles. By offering commuter benefits, including carpooling and vanpooling, a company with 1,000 employees can lower its annual parking expenses by more than $70,000 and save participating employees $13,000 each year in taxes and $160,000 each year in gasoline, parking, and vehicle costs.

How long does this take to implement?
A vanpooling/carpooling program can be implemented within a few months. Once the program is established, individual pools can be set up in less than a few weeks.

The Bottom Line
Carpooling and vanpooling commuters get to work in ways that reduce air pollution and traffic congestion, save employers and employees money, reduce the environmental impacts associated with driving single-passenger vehicles, reduce parking space demand and expenses, and relieve commuter stress.

Who needs to be involved?
- Governing board and/or management (to endorse a vanpool/carpool policy and support a program that provides incentives for employees who participate in a vanpool or carpool)
- Businesses and their human resource or fiscal office staff
- Transit providers and/or private vanpool leasing companies
- Private parking deck and lot owners
- Employees willing to start up their own vanpool or carpool

(*Source:* Used with permission from Sustainable Environment for Quality of Life, www.seql.org)

GOAL ➤ **Interpret information about environmental issues**

D Working with a partner, choose one of the following three environmental topics. Come up with a list of programs that might work to improve the environment in your community.

air quality   water resources   sustainable development

Topic: _____

Possible programs: _____

_____

_____

_____

E Find another pair of students who chose the same topic as you. Work together and share your ideas. Then, choose one program to develop. Think about and decide on the following items.

Topic: _____

Name of program: _____

Briefly describe how program works: _____

_____

_____

_____

Impact and benefit the environment: _____

_____

_____

Length of time to implement: _____

Cost: _____

People involved: _____

Expressing yourself

GOAL ➤ **Communicate your opinion**

A Everyone has an opinion when it comes to the environment. In a small group, brainstorm some *yes* and *no* opinions for each of the suggestions below.

EXAMPLE: People should not be permitted to buy large cars that create a lot of pollution.

Yes: *If everyone bought smaller cars, pollution would be significantly reduced.*

No: *Many people need large cars for their families. Large cars are safer and hold more people and more groceries.*

1. Our city should build more carpool lanes.

Yes	No
a. _____	a. _____
b. _____	b. _____
c. _____	c. _____

2. Everyone should take his own recyclable items to a recycling center.

Yes	No
a. _____	a. _____
b. _____	b. _____
c. _____	c. _____

3. Each home should only be allowed to have a certain amount of water per month.

Yes	No
a. _____	a. _____
b. _____	b. _____
c. _____	c. _____

B Practice communicating your opinion to a partner.

EXAMPLE: **A:** *I think our city should build more carpool lanes.*
B: *I disagree. In my opinion, it is a waste of money because it won't make more people carpool.*

> **Phrases for Communicating Your Opinion**
> I think . . .   I believe . . .   In my opinion, . . .   I agree.   I disagree.

C Ella wrote a paragraph communicating her opinion on the environment. Read.

Our Most Precious Resource

There are many things we should do to protect our environment, but I think one of the most important things we can do is to conserve water. Why? Water is one of our most precious resources. I believe this for many reasons. One reason is that the human body is made up of 75% water. We can only live for one week without water; therefore, we need to drink water to survive. Another reason that water is so important is that we need it to clean. We need water to clean our bodies, wash our dishes, flush our toilets, and launder our clothes. Can you imagine not being able to do any of these things? Still another reason is that plants and trees need water to grow and survive. Without plants and trees, humans wouldn't survive because plants give off the oxygen we need in order to breathe. For these reasons, I believe that we need to conserve our most precious resource—water.

D Answer the questions about the sentence types in Ella's paragraph.

1. What is Ella's topic sentence?

_____

2. What is Ella's concluding sentence?

_____

3. Ella gives three reasons to support her main idea. For each idea, she gives a supporting detail. What are her reasons and details?

a. Reason: _____

   Detail: _____

b. Reason: _____

   Detail: _____

c. Reason: _____

   Detail: _____

E   Study these transitional expressions with your teacher. Which ones did Ella use in her paragraph?

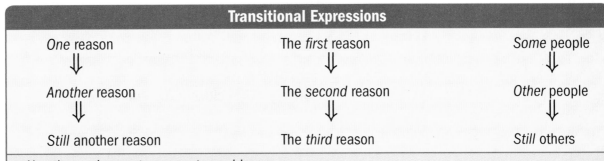

Transitional Expressions

One reason
⇓
Another reason
⇓
Still another reason

The *first* reason
⇓
The *second* reason
⇓
The *third* reason

Some people
⇓
Other people
⇓
Still others

- Use these phrases to connect your ideas.
- Choose the set of phrases that works best for your topic.
- Don't shift back and forth among sets of phrases.

F   What are some of your ideas about the environment? Use a cluster map like this one to brainstorm your ideas.

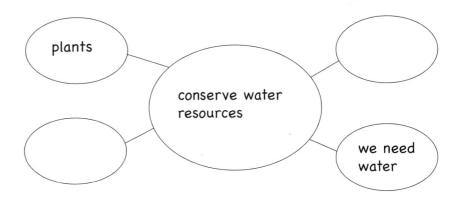

G   Choose one of your ideas. Write three reasons to support that idea.

Reason 1: _____

Reason 2: _____

Reason 3: _____

H   Come up with at least one detail to support each reason.

Detail 1: _____

Detail 2: _____

Detail 3: _____

I   On a separate piece of paper, write a paragraph communicating your opinion about the environment.

Review

A List four ways one can become a permanent resident of the United States. (Lesson 1)

1. _____
2. _____
3. _____
4. _____

B List four requirements for becoming a U.S. citizen. (Lesson 1)

1. _____
2. _____
3. _____
4. _____

C Write the correct amendment number in front of each description. (Lesson 2)

1. The _____ amendment is about the abolishment of slavery.

2. The _____ amendment is about the right for women to vote.

3. The _____ amendment is about the right to be charged by a grand jury if accused of a serious crime.

4. The _____ amendment is about protection from unreasonable search and seizure.

5. The _____ amendment is about a trial by jury in civil cases (dispute between private parties or between the government and a private party).

6. The _____ amendment is about a speedy and public trial by an impartial jury.

7. The _____ amendment is about freedom of religion.

8. The _____ amendment is about the right to keep and bear arms.

9. The _____ amendment is about the right for people of all races to vote.

10. The _____ amendment is about protection from forced housing of soldiers.

D Create a civic organization for the following group's problem. (Lesson 3)

A group of children who live in a shelter for homeless families goes to a nearby elementary school. However, the parents of the children don't have any money to buy the required school uniform—blue pants and a white shirt. The volunteers at the shelter want to find a way to raise money for these kids.

Name of organization: _____

Purpose: _____

Members: _____

Annual dues: _____

Special events: _____

E Work with a partner and list ten ways you can help protect and preserve the environment. (Lesson 4)

1. _____   6. _____

2. _____   7. _____

3. _____   8. _____

4. _____   9. _____

5. _____   10. _____

F Choose one of the ways you and your partner listed in Exercise E and write a paragraph about why it is important. (Lesson 5)

_____

_____

_____

_____

_____

_____

_____

VOCABULARY REVIEW

alien	conserve	protect	reusable
bear arms	eligible	punishment	slavery
believe	naturalization	refugee	social welfare
capital crime	opinion	resource	status
civic	peaceably assemble		

G Choose five words from the vocabulary list above. Use each word in a meaningful sentence that reviews an important point or piece of information that you have learned in this unit.

1. _____

2. _____

3. _____

4. _____

5. _____

H Use five different words from the list above to write five different opinions you have.

1. _____

2. _____

3. _____

4. _____

5. _____

I Write the correct word in front of each definition below.

1. _____ means resident foreigner.

2. _____ means having the right to do or be chosen for something.

3. _____ means a payment for doing something wrong.

4. _____ means useful things.

5. _____ means a legal condition.

Research Project

A Think about the things you have learned in this unit. Imagine that you want to know more about something you have learned. What would be the best way to research it? Write your ideas next to each topic.

1. Becoming a resident or citizen: _____

   _____

2. The Bill of Rights: _____

   _____

3. Civic organizations: _____

   _____

4. Environmental issues: _____

   _____

B Choose one of the topics from Exercise A that you want to research. Make a list of what you want to know more about or questions you want answered.

I want to know . . .

1. _____

2. _____

3. _____

4. _____

5. _____

C Research your topic and find the information in your want-to-know list above. Take notes on a separate piece of paper.

D Share what you learned with your classmates.

Individual Project

Give an opinion speech.

In this project, you will work <u>individually</u> to develop an opinion speech supported with details.

1. Look back at everything you have learned in this unit and choose one topic to give a speech about. Remember, this speech should be persuasive. You should not just present facts without giving your opinion. However, you can support your opinion with facts. First, write one sentence that states your opinion.

   Some examples:

   • *I think that someone should be able to become a citizen anytime he or she wants.*

   • *I don't think Americans should have the right to bear arms.*

   • *I think every citizen should have to be a part of a civic organization.*

2. Read your opinion out loud to the class.

3. Come up with reasons to support your opinion and write a speech. Prepare to speak for at least two minutes.

4. Practice your speech. Remember the following tips:

   • Annunciate (speak clearly).

   • Make eye contact with your audience.

   • Practice so you recall your major points without notes.

   • Thank your audience for listening and/or for their time.

5. Give your two-minute opinion speech. At the end of your speech, ask your classmates if they have any questions.

Photo Credits

Stand Out 5 Goals Checklist

➤ Think about your knowledge of the goals listed below.
➤ Check if you achieved this goal during the unit.
➤ Write the page number(s) for the goals that you still need to review.
➤ As you work through the text, make a list of your own personal goals.

Pre-Unit: Getting to Know You

Goals	Achieved	Page(s)
Get to know my classmates	☐ Yes ☐ Maybe ☐ No	
Talk about personal interests	☐ Yes ☐ Maybe ☐ No	
Write a personal letter	☐ Yes ☐ Maybe ☐ No	

Unit 1: Balancing Your Life

Goals	Achieved	Page(s)
Identify my learning style	☐ Yes ☐ Maybe ☐ No	
Identify a career path	☐ Yes ☐ Maybe ☐ No	
Balance my life	☐ Yes ☐ Maybe ☐ No	
Identify and prioritize goals	☐ Yes ☐ Maybe ☐ No	
Motivate myself	☐ Yes ☐ Maybe ☐ No	

Unit 2: Personal Finance

Goals	Achieved	Page(s)
Organize your finances	☐ Yes ☐ Maybe ☐ No	
Reduce debt and save money	☐ Yes ☐ Maybe ☐ No	
Identify investment strategies	☐ Yes ☐ Maybe ☐ No	
Maintain good credit	☐ Yes ☐ Maybe ☐ No	
Protect myself against identity theft	☐ Yes ☐ Maybe ☐ No	

Unit 3: Automotive Know-How

Goals	Achieved	Page(s)
Purchase a car	☐ Yes ☐ Maybe ☐ No	
Maintain and repair my car	☐ Yes ☐ Maybe ☐ No	
Interpret an auto insurance policy	☐ Yes ☐ Maybe ☐ No	
Compute mileage and gas consumption	☐ Yes ☐ Maybe ☐ No	
Follow the rules of the road	☐ Yes ☐ Maybe ☐ No	

Unit 4: Housing

Goals	Achieved	Page(s)
Communicate issues by phone	☐ Yes ☐ Maybe ☐ No	
Interpret rental agreements	☐ Yes ☐ Maybe ☐ No	
Identify tenant and landlord rights	☐ Yes ☐ Maybe ☐ No	
Get insurance	☐ Yes ☐ Maybe ☐ No	
Prevent theft	☐ Yes ☐ Maybe ☐ No	

Unit 5: Health

Goals	Achieved	Page(s)
Identify practices that promote mental and physical well-being	☐ Yes ☐ Maybe ☐ No	
Ask about medical bills	☐ Yes ☐ Maybe ☐ No	
Interpret health insurance information	☐ Yes ☐ Maybe ☐ No	
Identify addictions	☐ Yes ☐ Maybe ☐ No	
Interpret procedures for first aid	☐ Yes ☐ Maybe ☐ No	

Unit 6: Retail

Goals	Achieved	Page(s)
Do product research	☐ Yes ☐ Maybe ☐ No	
Purchase goods and services by phone and Internet	☐ Yes ☐ Maybe ☐ No	
Interpret product guarantees and warranties	☐ Yes ☐ Maybe ☐ No	
Return a product	☐ Yes ☐ Maybe ☐ No	
Sell a product	☐ Yes ☐ Maybe ☐ No	

Unit 7: The Office

Goals	Achieved	Page(s)
Identify and use technology	☐ Yes ☐ Maybe ☐ No	
Resolve technological problems	☐ Yes ☐ Maybe ☐ No	
Establish an organizational system	☐ Yes ☐ Maybe ☐ No	
Identify and resolve problems at work	☐ Yes ☐ Maybe ☐ No	
Report progress	☐ Yes ☐ Maybe ☐ No	

Unit 8: Civic Responsibility

Goals	Achieved	Page(s)
Identify requirements for establishing residency and citizenship	☐ Yes ☐ Maybe ☐ No	
Understand my rights	☐ Yes ☐ Maybe ☐ No	
Identify local civic organizations	☐ Yes ☐ Maybe ☐ No	
Interpret information about environmental issues	☐ Yes ☐ Maybe ☐ No	
Communicate my opinion	☐ Yes ☐ Maybe ☐ No	

My Personal Goals	To Achieve By (Date)

Vocabulary List

Pre-Unit
cook, P5
do crossword puzzles, P5
do yoga, P5
draw, P5
knit, P5
lift weights, P5
paint, P5
play soccer, P5
play video games, P5
read, P5
run, P5
swim, P5
take pictures, P5
watch movies, P5
write, P5

Unit 1
achieve, 2, 20
auditory, 1, 2
balance, 2, 20
be flexible, 2, 20
bodily, 2, 6
career path, 1, 2
computer programmer, 1
earning power, 2, 20
educational attainment, 2, 20
evaluate, 2, 20
financial, 1
fun, 1
goal setting, 2
graphic designer, 1
inspire, 2, 20
intelligences, 2
interpersonal, 2, 6
intrapersonal, 2, 6
joy, 1
kinesthetic, 2, 6
learning style, 1, 2
linguistic, 2, 6
logical, 2, 6
long-term, 2, 20
mathematical, 6
monitor, 2, 20
motivate, 2, 20
motivation, 1, 2
multiple, 2
musical, 6
naturalistic, 2, 6
photographer, 1
positive outlook, 2, 20
prioritize, 2, 20
pursue, 2, 20
registered nurse, 1
rhythmic, 2, 6
short-term, 2, 20
spatial, 2, 6

support, 2, 20
tactile, 1, 2
time with family, 1
verbal, 2, 6
visual, 1, 2, 6

Unit 2
bankruptcy, 24
bargain, 42
budget cut, 23
buy in bulk, 23
capital gains, 23, 31
collateral, 24
commit fraud, 23
convert, 31, 42
counterfeit, 42
counterfeit checks, 23
current income, 23
daunting, 24
debt, 42
delinquent, 42
delinquent accounts, 23
dumpster diving, 37
earnings, 42
expense, 42
false pretenses, 23
fraud, 42
inflation, 24, 31
investment, 24
liquid, 24, 31
net appreciation, 31
penalty, 24, 31
periodically, 24
phishing, 37
pretexting, 37
purchasing power, 31
risk, 42
risky, 24, 31
skimming, 37
unauthorized transactions, 23
value, 31
vehicle, 31
worth, 42

Unit 3
accident, 46
air filter, 50
alternator, 50
battery, 50
bodily injury, 46
brake fluid reservoir, 50
change, 46, 62
check, 62
children, 59
choose, 46
collision, 46, 64
commute, 46
convertible, 45

coolant reservoir, 50
coverage, 46
disc brake, 50
distributor, 50
do, 46
exhaust manifold, 50
fatalities, 64
fill, 62
fill up, 46
find, 46
four-door sedan, 45
fuel injection system, 50
imagine, 46
incident, 46
inspect, 62
limits of liability, 46
look at, 46
make, 46
minivan, 45
model, 46
MPG, 64
muffler, 50
odometer, 64
pedestrians, 59
perform, 62
pickup truck, 45
police officer, 59
policy, 46
power steering reservoir, 50
premium, 46, 64
radiator, 50
rear axle, 50
rear suspension, 50
red light, 59
replace, 46, 62
school bus, 59
seat belts, 59
speed limit, 59
sports car, 45
sport utility vehicle (SUV), 45
station wagon, 45
stop sign, 59
timing belt, 50
top off, 62
two-door coupe, 45
uninsured motorist, 46
unrestrained, 64
van, 45
VIN, 46
water pump, 50

Unit 4
abandon, 67
activate, 68
burglarize, 67
burglary, 86
compensate, 68

Review: *Be*			
Subject	*Past*	**Present**	**Future**
I	was	am	will be
you	were	are	will be
he, she, it	was	is	will be
we	were	are	will be
they	were	are	will be

Review: Simple Tenses				
Subject	**Past**	**Present**	**Future**	
I	spent	spend	will spend	more time with my brothers.
You	enjoyed	enjoy	will enjoy	being a mother.
He, She, It	studied	studies	will study	English every day.
We	put	put	will put	our studies first.
They	worked	work	will work	too many hours.

Future Perfect Tense				
Subject	*will have*	**Past participle**		**Future event—Time expression**
I	will have	become	a teacher	by the time my kids are in school.
He	will have	been	a graphic designer (for five years)	when he turns 35.
They	will have	found	a job	by 2015.

We use the future perfect to talk about an activity that will be completed before another time or event in the future. ——————|—— present ——✕—— future to be completed (perfect) ——✕—— future event with time expression ——————

Note: The order of events is not important. If the future event with the time expression comes first, use a comma.

Example: *By the time my kids are in school, I will have become a teacher.*

Past Perfect Continuous Tense

First event in past					Second event in past
Subject	*had*	*been*	**Verb + -ing**		
Kimla	had	been	buying	designer clothes	before she started bargain shopping.
He	had	been	buying	coffee at a coffee shop	before he began making it at home.
They	had	been	paying	a lower deductible	before they called the insurance company.

- We use the past perfect continuous to talk about an activity that was happening for a while before another event happened in the past. For the most recent event, we use the simple past tense.

- Remember to use a comma if you put the second event as the first part of the sentence.
  Example: Before she started bargain shopping, Kimla had been buying designer clothes.

Causative Verbs: *Get, Have, Help, Make, Let*

Subject	Verb	Noun/Pronoun	Infinitive (Omit *to* except with *get.*)
He	will get	his handyman	to come.
She	had	her mom	wait for the repairperson.
The landlord	helped	me	move in.
Ming Mei	makes	her sister	pay half of the rent.
Mr. Martin	let	Ming Mei	skip one month's rent.

Adverb Clauses of Concession

Dependent clause	Independent clause
Although he spends a lot of time in Las Vegas,	he says he doesn't have a gambling problem.
Even though her sister spends thousands of dollars a month,	she doesn't think she is a shopaholic.
Though she has to drink two cups of coffee before she can get out of bed in the morning,	she is convinced she isn't addicted to caffeine.
In spite of the fact that he plays video games for three hours a night,	he denies he has a problem.

Explanation: Adverb clauses of concession show a contrast in ideas. The main or independent clauses show the unexpected outcome. The unexpected outcome in the third example is that it is surprising that she thinks she isn't addicted to caffeine.

Note: The clauses can be reversed and have the same meaning. Do not use a comma if the independent clause comes first in the sentence.

Example: *She doesn't think she is a shopaholic even though she spends thousands of dollars a month.*

Appositives

Noun or Noun Phrase	Appositive	Remainder of sentence (Predicate)
The ad,	**the one with all the great pictures,**	makes me want to buy those dishes.
That computer,	**the fastest machine in the store,**	sells for over $2,000.

Explanation:
- An appositive is a noun or noun phrase that renames another noun next to it in a sentence.
- The appositive adds extra descriptive detail, explains, or identifies something about the noun.

Example: *A helpful gift, money is always appreciated by a newly married couple.*
- An appositive can come before or after the noun phrase it is modifying:

Note: Appositives are usually set off by commas.

Noun Clauses as Objects

Subject + Verb	Noun clause	Explanation
I did	*what* I was asked.	· A noun clause starts with a question word or *that* and is followed by a subject and verb.
She knows	*how* the computer works.	
They decided	*where* the location would be.	· In these examples, the noun clauses are the objects of the sentences.
My boss asked	*who* would be best for the job.	
I hope	*that* they work as a team.	

Transitional Expressions

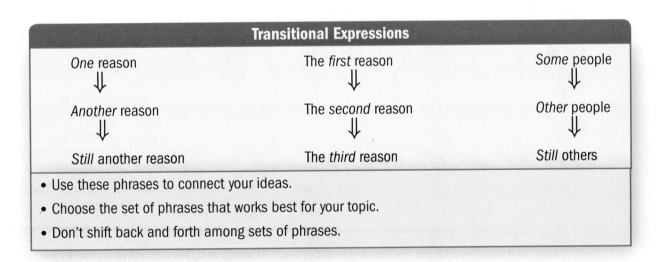

- Use these phrases to connect your ideas.
- Choose the set of phrases that works best for your topic.
- Don't shift back and forth among sets of phrases.

Stand Out 5 Listening Scripts

PRE-UNIT
CD, Track 1, Page P1
A. Read and listen to the conversation between Liam and Rani. Do you know people like them?

Liam: Hi, my name is Liam. I am from France.

Rani: Nice to meet you, Liam. My name is Rani and I'm from India.

Liam: Nice to meet you, Rani. Why are you studying English?

Rani: I have been here for over 20 years. I stay home and help take care of my grandchildren while their parents work. But I finally decided to improve my English so I can help them with their schoolwork. What about you?

Liam: I moved here so I could study at a university and learn how to be a graphic designer.

CD, Track 2, Page P2
D. Read and listen to the conversation between Liam, Rani, and Haru. What does Liam say to introduce Haru to Rani?

Liam: Rani, I'd like you to meet Haru. He is from Japan and came here last year.

Rani: It's a pleasure to meet you, Haru. You seem very young!

Haru: Actually, I just finished high school, but my English writing still isn't good enough to go to college, so I'm going to study for one more year before I apply.

Rani: Oh, that's smart. You remind me of my son. We came here when he was in high school, too.

CD, Track 3, Page P3
G. Read and listen to Haru introduce Kimla to the class.

Haru: I'd like you to meet Kimla. She came here with her family from Saudi Arabia four years ago. She has been studying English for three years now and would like to become a registered nurse. She hopes to apply to a nursing program at the end of this semester.

Class: Nice to meet you, Kimla.

CD, Track 4, Page P4
B. Listen to the conversation between Haru, Rani, and Kimla. Then, answer the questions below.

Haru: So, Mrs. Morgan wants us to talk about our personal interests. What do you think she means by "personal interests"?

Rani: I think she means, "What do we like to do when we are not in school or not working?"

Kimla: I think you're right, Rani. When I'm not working or in school, I like to read. Not school books but fiction and biographies, newspapers, magazines, anything I can get my hands on. Sometimes I'm up until two in the morning, just reading.

Haru: Wow, that's impressive! I hate reading, which made it pretty hard to get through my last year of high school. I like to play video games. Just like you can read for hours, I can sit and stare at a TV screen for hours, playing games. My favorite kind of games are adventure where you have to solve problems to get to the next place.

Rani: I know I've said it before, but you remind me so much of my son. He likes video games, too. Although now that he has a family, he doesn't get to play them as much any more. In my free time, I like to take pictures. My son and his wife gave me a new SLR digital camera, and it takes such amazing pictures! My favorite type of photography is nature photography, so I'm outdoors a lot.

Kimla: That's great, Rani. The three of us have such varied interests. It's so fun to hear about what other people do when they aren't in school.

UNIT 1
CD, Track 5, Page 3
B. Listen to a lecturer talk about the three learning styles and take notes. Write down any key words you hear to describe each learning style.

Do you learn best through seeing? Then you are a visual learner. Visual learners learn from body language and facial expressions.

They like to sit in the front of the classroom so they can see clearly. They tend to think in pictures and learn best by looking at visuals, such as diagrams, pictures, overheads, videos, and handouts. Visual learners like to take detailed notes to help learn information.

Do you learn best by listening? Then you are an auditory learner. Auditory learners learn best by listening to lectures, participating in discussions, and listening to what others say. They also listen to tone of voice, pitch and speed to interpret hidden meanings. Auditory learners learn best if they read text aloud.

Do you like to learn by moving, doing, and touching? Then you are a tactile or kinesthetic learner. Kinesthetic learners like to actively explore their surroundings by touching things and moving. They have trouble sitting still for long periods of time. They learn best through a hands-on approach.

CD, Track 6, Page 8
H. Listen to the conversation between a school counselor and Sonya. Take notes on the information you hear.

Counselor: Hi, Sonya. How are you today?

Sonya: A bit tired. Taking care of the kids and going to school is keeping me quite busy!

Counselor: I'll bet. I remember those days. Even though you get tired sometimes, doing both of those things is so worthwhile.

Sonya: I know it is. I just have to keep reminding myself of that!

Counselor: Well, based on what we talked about in our last meeting, I would say your intelligences are most likely interpersonal as well as verbal and linguistic. Now based on that list of careers that we looked at, are there any that seem interesting to you?

Sonya: Actually, teacher kept jumping out at me. It showed up on the list for both of those intelligences. I have always loved working with children and helping them learn new things.

Counselor: Well, I think that sounds like a great career for you . . . elementary school teacher. Have you ever thought about doing that before?

Sonya: Not really. I never thought my English would be good enough to be a teacher. And I didn't think I could get into a school to earn a degree.

Counselor: Well, you are wrong on both counts. You have worked really hard and your English is getting better every day. And there are plenty of schools that would be happy to accept you as an education major.

Sonya: Will it be expensive?

Counselor: That all depends on what school you choose. But you can start at a city or community college to get your general education requirements done and then, you can transfer to a four-year school to finish up your degree and get your teaching credentials. That will definitely keep the costs down.

Sonya: How long will it take?

Counselor: Well, that all depends on you. If you can go to school full time, you could finish in four years. And I know you have little ones at home, so we can look around for some schools that offer some online classes so you can study on your own time.

Sonya: I'll have to talk to my husband to see if he still needs me to work part time.

Counselor: If you have to, there's no reason why you couldn't still work. It will just take you a little bit longer to get your degree.

Sonya: I wouldn't mind that. I don't want a full-time teaching job until both of my kids are in school anyways.

Counselor: That's smart. Your girls will appreciate having you home with them.

Sonya: So what's the next step?

Counselor: Well, since you already have your high school diploma, let's start looking around at some local colleges where you can do your general education requirements. I'll put together a list for you and then, we can do some research on what English level you need to be at before you can apply.

Sonya: Sounds great. Thank you so much for all your help!

CD, Track 7, Page 9
A. Sonya has many roles. Listen to her and take notes.
Sonya: I am a wife. I am a mother. I am a sister. I am a student. I am a friend. I am a manager. I was a secretary. I will be an elementary school teacher.

CD, Track 8, Page 13
C. Listen to the lecture on goal setting and take notes below.
Goal setting is a process that makes you think about your future and helps motivate you to make that future a reality. Setting goals helps you choose the direction you want your life to go in. As you set and achieve goals, your self-confidence will improve.

The first thing you should do is create a big picture of where you want to be in a certain number of years. Once you have created your big picture, you can make smaller or short-term goals.

In this workshop, we'd like you to focus on seven different types of goals. First are educational goals. Is there anything special you want or need to learn? Or is there any degree you need to get to pursue your career goals? Second are career goals. How far would you like to go in your career? Third are financial goals. How much money would you like to be earning? Fourth are attitude goals. Would you like to change the way you think or act? Fifth are family goals. Do you want to have a family, increase the size of your family, or improve some of your family relationships? Sixth are physical goals. Is there anything you'd like to do to improve your health? Would you like to enter a physical competition? And finally, pleasure goals. Are there any hobbies you'd like to do? It is important to enjoy your life so make sure you think about goals for pleasure.

It is important to spend some time thinking about all these different goals, and try to choose one goal in each category that best reflects what you want to do. Then, you should prioritize these goals and focus on a small number of goals at one time.

So, how do you go about setting these goals? Here are five tips that should help you to set effective goals:
1. Set realistic goals. It is important to set a goal that you can actually achieve. It will lower your self-confidence if you set goals that are unrealistic.
2. Write down your goals. Writing your goals down gives them life. Try to put them in a place where you will see them every day.
3. Write each goal as a positive statement.
4. Be precise. When you set your goals, write down exact times, dates, etc. This way, it will be easy to see when you have achieved a goal.
5. Prioritize. When you have more than one goal, put them in order of importance. This will help you direct your attention to the most important goals and avoid feeling overwhelmed by having too much to do.

So now that we talked about types of goals and tips for setting these goals, should we get down to business?

CD, Track 9, Page 15
C. Listen to Mrs. Morgan's students talk about motivating themselves. Take notes about what each person says.
Liam: I told my friends and family about my goals so they could support me.
Haru: I keep a chart up in my room of the goals I have reached and the ones I still need to reach. When I reach a goal, I put a sticker on the chart.
Kimla: I made a list of all my goals and I keep it taped inside my planner, so I see it every day.
Sonya: I read books and look for articles on the Internet to inspire me.
Rani: I remind myself every morning to have a positive attitude. I tell myself, "I can do it!"
Mario: I set very small goals, so that I can get excited every time I achieve one.

UNIT 2
CD, Track 10, Page 25
C. Listen to a financial planner talking about how to organize personal finances. Write down the most important points the planner makes.

Counselor: Let's get started. The first thing you need to do is go through all of your bank statements, credit card statements, receipts — basically all of the financial paperwork you have for the past year. Next, write down all of the categories in which you spend money. Then, figure out how much you spent in each category each month. Fourth, add up how much you spent each month to find out how much you spend per year in each category. Finally, total up all those annual numbers and divide the total by 12 to find out how much you spend each month on average. If you do all these things, you'll find you'll have a good idea of your annual or yearly expenses.

CD, Track 11, Page 29
D. Listen to Kimla and her husband, Derek, talk about saving money. Write T (true) or F (false) on the line before each statement.
Kimla: Derek, I really think we need to come up with some more ways to save money.
Derek: More? I thought we were doing really well with our money. I'm really proud of myself for making my own coffee instead of buying it at a coffee shop and now I'm clipping coupons, too.
Kimla: Yes, you are doing a great job. But weren't you supposed to buy a used car? I thought you were looking at used cars, but then you ended up buying a new one.
Derek: Well, what about you and your designer clothes?
Kimla: At least I started buying generic name products and turning off the air conditioner before I go to bed.
Derek: Um, what about your designer clothes?
Kimla: I know, I know, I used to be so good at looking for bargains. But I just love the designer fashions. At least I was able to call the credit card companies and lower our interest rates, so we are no longer paying on high interest cards.
Derek: Yeah, that was a good move. And I called the insurance company to increase our deductible, so our premiums would go down.
Kimla: I guess you're right, Derek. We are doing a pretty good job.
Derek: Yep, I agree.

CD, Track 12, Page 37
A. Listen to each of the following people talk about their financial problems. What happened? Take notes on the lines below each photo.
Man 1: I was looking over my credit card statement last night and I noticed some charges from unfamiliar companies. When I called the companies to see what the charges were for, I found out that they were companies that I had never done business with. Apparently someone had gotten my credit card number off of the Internet and had been using it for months to make online purchases.
Man 2: My cell phone bill was really expensive this month. When I looked closer, I realized that I had been charged for a phone number that wasn't mine. When I called the phone company to dispute it, they said that I had indeed called and added a line to my account. I told them this wasn't true and we discovered that someone had stolen my personal information and added a phone line to my account.
Woman: I was in the supermarket the other day and when I tried to pay for my groceries with my ATM card, it was declined due to insufficient funds. So then I went to an ATM machine and the same thing happened. I called my bank and found out that someone in another state had gotten a copy of my ATM card and had withdrawn all of the money.

CD, Track 13, Page 38
D. Listen to an interview with a member of the Federal Trade Commission (FTC). In each question below, one answer is NOT correct. Choose the incorrect answer.
Identity theft occurs when someone uses your personally identifying information, such as your name, Social Security number, or credit card number without your permission to commit fraud or other crimes.

The FTC estimates that as many as nine million Americans have their identities stolen each year. In fact, you or someone you know may have experienced some form of identity theft. Identity theft is serious. While some identity theft victims can resolve their problems quickly, others spend hundreds of dollars and many days repairing damage to their good name and credit record.

How do thieves steal an identity?
Identity theft starts with the misuse of your personal identification information, such as your name and Social Security number, credit card numbers, or other financial account information. Skilled identity thieves may use a variety of methods to get hold of your information, including: dumpster diving, skimming, and phishing. When thieves dumpster dive, they rummage through trash looking for bills or other paper with your personal information on it. When thieves employ the skimming method, they steal credit or debit card numbers by using a special storage device when processing your card. If thieves are phishing, they pretend to be financial institutions or companies and send spam or pop-up messages to get you to reveal your personal information.

Often thieves change your address by completing a change-of-address form and they then divert your billing statements to another location. Identity thieves also use forms of old-fashioned methods, such as stealing wallets and purses; mail, including bank and credit card statements; pre-approved credit offers; and new checks or tax information. They steal personnel records or bribe employees who have access to them. Thieves also use false pretenses to obtain your personal information from financial institutions, telephone companies, and other sources.

What do thieves do with a stolen identity? Once they have your personal information, identity thieves use it in a variety of ways.
Credit card fraud: They may open new credit card accounts in your name. When they use the cards and don't pay the bills, the delinquent accounts appear on your credit report. They may change the billing address on your credit card so that you no longer receive bills, and then run up charges on your account. Because your bills are now sent to a different address, it may be some time before you realize there's a problem. **Phone or utilities fraud:** They may open a new phone or wireless account in your name, or run up charges on your existing account. They may use your name to get utility services like electricity, heating, or cable TV. **Bank/finance fraud:** They may create counterfeit checks using your name or account number. They may open a bank account in your name and write bad checks. They may clone your ATM or debit card and make electronic withdrawals in your name, draining your accounts. They may take out a loan in your name.
Government documents fraud: They may get a driver's license or official ID card issued in your name, but with their picture. They may use your name and Social Security number to get government benefits. They may file a fraudulent tax return using your information. **Other fraud:** They may get a job using your Social Security number. They may rent a house or get medical services using your name. They may give your personal information to police during an arrest. If they don't show up for their court date, a warrant for arrest is issued in your name.

How can you find out if your identity was stolen? The best way to find out is to monitor your accounts and bank statements each month, and check your credit report on a regular basis. If you check your credit report regularly, you may be able to limit the damage caused by identity theft.

What should you do if your identity is stolen? Filing a police report, checking your credit reports, notifying creditors, and disputing any unauthorized transactions are some of the steps you must take immediately to restore your good name.

What can you do to help fight identity theft? A great deal. Awareness is an effective weapon against many forms of identity theft. Be aware of how information is stolen and what you can do

to protect yours, monitor your personal information to uncover any problems quickly, and know what to do when you suspect your identity has been stolen. You can also help fight identity theft by educating your friends, family, and members of your community.

UNIT 3
CD, Track 14, Page 47
B. Listen to an auto salesman who is trying to sell you a car. Take notes on what he says about the different kinds of cars.
Well, since you don't know what kind of car you are looking for, let me tell you about all the different types of vehicle on the market. Then, you can decide which one will be best suited to you.
First, let's talk about 4-Door Sedans—Sedans are a good choice for most automobile shoppers. The enclosed trunk offers security, while the rear doors allow easy entry for rear-seat passengers. Most luxury vehicles are four-door sedans because they're more comfortable than most other body styles. **A smaller car is a 2-Door Coupe**—Coupes are usually driven by single adults or childless couples. Many of them have a hatchback instead of a trunk, to allow large items to be carried for short distances. The rear seats are difficult to access, as the front doors must be used. **A larger car is a Station Wagon**—An active family will want to look at minivans, sport utility vehicles, or station wagons. In most of the world, station wagons remain the first choice for active families. Station wagons offer more stability, better gas mileage, lower insurance rates, and SUV-sized interiors. You won't lose your all-wheel drive either, as Subaru, Volkswagen, Audi, Volvo, and Mercedes-Benz offer all-wheel drive on all of their wagons. **Let's talk about a fun car, a Convertible**—Most convertibles are sports cars, meaning two seats, high-performance engines and superior handling. However, GM, Ford, Mitsubishi, and Chrysler offer a few "normal" convertibles, that is, regular production coupes with four seats and convertible tops, such as the Chevrolet Cavalier, Pontiac Sunfire, Ford Mustang, Dodge Avenger, Chrysler Conquest, and Mitsubishi Eclipse Spyder. Luxury convertibles are available from BMW, Mercedes-Benz, Saab, and Volvo. Convertibles are great when the weather's perfect, but their drawbacks are obvious. **And even more fun (and more expensive) Sports Cars**—Sports cars were originally European two-seat roadsters designed for both daily travel and week-end racing hobbyists. The term sports-sedan is a more recent term to describe a four-door vehicle that handles like a sports coupe or roadster. Recently we've seen luxury cars advertised as luxury sports sedans. Sports cars are cool and fun to drive, though impractical for daily transportation. You'll need a garage to store them in, and a second mortgage to pay for their insurance. But if you've got money to burn, go for it! **Then there's the Minivan**—If you're constantly carting kids or cargo, a minivan may be your best choice. Most new models offer an additional fourth door on the driver's side and offer comfortable seating for seven. Minivans drive and handle just like a car, with the bonus of better visibility due to a higher center of gravity and an upright driving position. Don't look for minivans to handle your boat or trailer towing duties, as front-wheel drive vehicles have a very limited towing capacity. **One of the most popular cars out there right now is the Sport Utility Vehicles (SUVs)**—Although they're designed for off-road usage, 98% of them never leave the road, fortunately for our wildernesses. If a wagon isn't for you, the car-like SUV rides and handles significantly better than the rest. Unfortunately they guzzle a lot of gas, so you may want to think twice before buying one. **My personal favorite is the Pickup Truck**—More new pickup trucks are sold in this country than any other type of vehicle. The smaller models now offer quad or crew-cab four-door versions, with seating for five adults. Full-size models offer extended cabs with smaller third and fourth doors giving access to the rear seats. Standard rear-wheel drive versions don't handle well on snow or ice without a substantial amount of weight in the rear of the truck. When equipped with towing packages with

8- or 10-cylinder engines, these rear-wheel drive vehicles can tow large boats and trailers. Full-size 2-wheel and 4-wheel drive pickups get about 15 miles per gallon. **A little less common, but necessary if you're transporting a lot of people is a Van**—If you transport large amounts of cargo or need room for more than seven adults, a full-size van is your only option. They're available with and without windows and in payload capacities of over one ton. Extended vans can seat up to 15 adult passengers. Towing packages with 8- or 10-cylinder engines will allow these rear-wheel-drive vehicles to tow large boats and trailers.
(Copyright 2002-2003 SafeCarGuide.com All rights reserved.)

CD, Track 15, Page 48

E. Rachel has decided to buy a car. She has been taking the bus and riding her bike everywhere so she has saved enough money to buy the car she wants. She has decided she wants a two-door coupe. Listen to what she did to research buying a car. Write down the different things she did.

Rachel: So, I finally decided that I want a two-door coupe. I think it will be the most economical for me because I am usually just driving myself to places. So, the first I made a list of all the two-door coupes for sale. Wow, there were a lot! Then, I called all my friends and family who own coupes and asked them which cars they had. I asked them what they liked and didn't like about their cars. Once I narrowed down my list, I went out to car dealerships two weekends in a row to test-drive cars. That really help me decide which ones I liked. At that point there were really only two cars that I liked. So, I went home and did some Internet research to find out where I could get the best prices. I also looked in the newspaper and the Autotrader to see what used cars might be available. I realized that I was going to get a lot more for my money if I bought a used car, and it seemed that the Autotrader had some pretty good deals. So, I called up a few people to test-drive their cars. I fell in love with one of them and brought my mechanic with me to take a look. He agreed that it was in great shape and a good price. Sold! I had my new car.

CD, Track 16, Page 56

A. Read and listen to the conversation between Keona and Chalene.

Keona: I can't believe the price of gasoline! I've been spending almost $60 just to fill up my tank.

Chalene: Same here. I've been trying to figure out how I can use my car less, so I save some money on gas.

Keona: Any good ideas?

Chalene: Well, I'm going to start carpooling to school two days a week, which should help. And I'm trying to combine my errands, so I only go out once a week.

Keona: That sounds good. I think I'm going to look into public transportation. I have a long drive to work, so maybe I can figure out how to take the train into town. I'll have to drive to the station and park but at least I won't be driving all the way to work.

Keona: That's great idea!

CD, Track 17, Page 57

D. In order to improve your gas mileage, you can follow certain maintenance tips. Listen and write the five tips you hear below.
Here are five tips that should help improve your gas mileage.

1. Get your engine tuned
An improperly tuned engine hurts gas mileage by an average of 4.1 percent, according to U.S. government studies. Most important to mileage is a properly working oxygen sensor, which helps keep your engine working efficiently.

2. Keep your tires properly inflated
Underinflated tires increase resistance and make it more difficult for the engine to move your car along the road. Check your tires every time you fill the tank. The U.S. Department of Energy estimates that people can improve their gas mileage by 3.3 percent by

inflating their tires regularly.

3. Check your air filter and replace it every 12,000 miles
Cars don't just run on gasoline. They actually run on gas and oxygen. If a clogged air filter restricts the flow of air, your performance and your fuel economy suffer. The Energy Department estimates that you could save as much as 22 cents per gallon by replacing a bad air filter.

4. Use the right motor oil.
Many people think it's OK to simply put any motor oil into the engine. While your motor will continue to work with a different grade of oil, it won't work quite as efficiently. You can save a couple cents per gallon by using the exact oil recommended for your car.

5. Don't carry junk in your trunk.
Get all those newspapers, cans and other baggage out of your car and trunk. Reducing the weight of the car increases mileage over the course of a tank of gas.
(www.edmunds.com)

UNIT 4
CD, Track 18, Page 69

A. Read and listen to the phone conversation Ming Mei is having with her landlord. What is the problem? How is the landlord going to fix it?

Landlord: Hello?

Ming Mei: Hi, Mr. Martin. This is Ming Mei from the apartment on Spring Street.

Landlord: Oh, hi, Ming Mei. What's up? Is there a problem?

Ming Mei: Well, after all the rain we had this weekend, the roof has started leaking. I think there may be a pool of water still on the roof because, even though it isn't raining anymore, there is still water leaking through our ceiling.

Landlord: Oh, no. Has it damaged the carpet?

Ming Mei: No, we caught it right away and put a bucket down to collect the drips.

Landlord: Oh, great. Thanks for being on top of it. I'll have my handyman come over and look at the roof and your ceiling. Can you let him in around 10 this morning?

Ming Mei: I have to go to work, but I can get my sister to come over.

Landlord: Great. Thanks for calling, Ming Mei.

Ming Mei: Thank you, Mr. Martin.

CD, Track 19, Page 69

C. Listen to the conversations between tenants and landlords. Take notes in the chart below.
Conversation 1

Landlord: Hello?

Chris: Hi, Mrs. Kashyap. This is Chris from your apartment building on Jerome Avenue.

Landlord: Oh, hi, Chris. What can I do for you?

Chris: Well, I was hoping you might be able to get the air-conditioning fixed. It's been so hot this summer.

Landlord: I know. It seems like I'm hearing the same thing from all of my tenants. The issue is, the repairman can't find the parts for that unit since it is so old. So, I think I'm going to have to get a new unit installed which could take me at least a month to do. In the meantime, I'm going to be dropping off some fans to all the tenants in your building. Would that be OK for now?

Chris: I guess so. When do you think you might come by?

Landlord: As soon as I can pick up those fans . . . before the end of the week. I'll call before I come.

Chris: OK. Thanks for your time, Mrs. Kashyap.

CD, Track 20, Page 69
Conversation 2

Landlord: Hello?

Janice: Hi, Mrs. Sawyer. This is Janice from Apartment 2B on Palo Verde.

Landlord: Oh, hi, Janice. How is everything going?

Janice: Pretty good. I was wondering if you might be able to fix the broken door handle on our bathroom. I know we talked about it when I moved in but it's been over three months and it still isn't fixed.

Landlord: Oh, thank you for calling and reminding me Janice. It completely slipped my mind. I'll send a handyman over first thing tomorrow.

Janice: Great, Mrs. Sawyer. Thanks!

CD, Track 21, Page 69
Conversation 3

Landlord: Hello, is this Mr. Jessup?

Mr. Jessup: Sure is.

Landlord: Hi, it's Mr. Little. I'm returning your call from yesterday.

Mr. Jessup: Oh, yes, Mr. Little. Thanks for calling back. It seems that the washing machine in our building isn't working. My wife was trying to do some laundry a few days ago and when she pulled the wet clothes out of the machine they were still full of soap.

Landlord: Oh, dear. That doesn't sound right.

Mr. Jessup: Actually, I think I know what the problem is. But I wanted to talk to you first before I went ahead and fixed it myself.

Landlord: Of course. If you think you can fix it, go right ahead. I'll deduct whatever it costs you from next month's rent.

Mr. Jessup: Great. I'll try to fix it this afternoon and I'll call you back to let you know if it's working again.

Landlord: Great, Mr. Jessup. Thanks for calling.

CD, Track 22, Page 78
A. Listen to Makela and Bryce talk about the renter's insurance quote below.

Makela: Hey Bryce, do you have renter's insurance?

Bryce: No. I keep thinking I need to get it, but I just haven't looked into it yet.

Makela: Well, I just call my insurance company and got a quote. Will you take a look at it and tell me what you think?

Bryce: How did they come up with this premium?

Makela: They asked a bunch of questions about the value of my personal belongings. Then, they came up with the dollar amount of what it would cost to replace all my stuff.

Bryce: What are the medical payments for?

Makela: In case someone gets hurt while they are at my apartment.

Bryce: And what about the liability?

Makela: Liability covers me if I cause any damage or physical harm to anyone. I think this is required as part of the insurance.

Bryce: Well, $18 a month sounds pretty reasonable to me. Would it cover your belongings if someone stole them?

Makela: Yep. It also covers disasters like fires or a flood. I think I'm going to sign up today. You should call too, Bryce.

Bryce: I think I will.

CD, Track 23, Page 83
E. Listen to the police officer talk about other tips to prevent break-ins. Write the tips below.

- Think like a burglar. "Case" your home the way a burglar would and look for easy ways to enter your home.
- Be sure valuables such as guns, electronic devices, and artwork are not visible from the street.
- Be sure to lock up ladders and tools, which could be used to break into your home.
- Work together with your neighbors. Organize a Neighborhood Watch and let your neighbors know when you will be away for an extended period.
- While on vacation, have someone pick up your newspapers and mail, so that they do not accumulate and alert burglars of your absence.
- Display your house number conspicuously and have it well illuminated. This will help police and emergency personnel find your home quickly.

(http://www.jcsd.org/burglary_prevention.htm)

CD, Track 24, Page 83
F. Sometimes, all your efforts will not stop a determined burglar. It's wise to take some precautions that will help you get your property back should a criminal successfully break into your home. Listen to the police officer and take notes.

- Make a list of your belongings (be sure to keep receipts, especially for expensive items like stereos and computers). Be sure to update this list periodically.
- Keep copies of your inventory list and receipts in a safe deposit box or with a friend. (This is also important in the event of a house fire.)
- Photographing and/or videotaping your possessions is a convenient way to keep a record of what you own.
- Engrave your valuables with an identification or mark to deter burglary and to prove ownership should the article be stolen and recovered by the police.
- Be sure you have the right coverage. You may need to purchase additional coverage to protect special items, like expensive jewelry or rare antiques.
- If you don't own your home, seriously consider buying a renter's policy. Your landlord will generally not be responsible for your possessions. Rental coverages are available at competitive rates and these policies also offer important protection against liability and losses due to fire or storm damage.

(http://www.jcsd.org/burglary_prevention.htm)

UNIT 5
CD, Track 25, Page 91
B. Listen to the following people talk about how they handle stress. Take notes.

Cooper: My name is Cooper and I work for a mortgage company. My job is very stressful because we work on commission, so they only way I get paid is by helping people refinance their homes. If I don't help one person, I don't make any money. The more people I help, the more money I make. I don't really like my job, so I'm going to school at night to study computer programming. So between work and school, I'm really busy and my work and studies put a lot of stress on me. One of the ways I cope with all this stress is meditation. Every morning before I leave for work, I sit outside on the porch where I can look at the trees and listen to the birds chirping. I close my eyes and breathe deeply, thinking of all the good things in my life. I picture my day at work as a productive, successful day. I picture my evening at school as a fun eye-opening experience where I learn many new things that will help me change careers. When I open my eyes, I feel refreshed and ready to take on the day.

Stephanie: My name is Stephanie. I cope with my stress by exercising. I run every night after work. Running gives me time to think and use up all that built up energy caused by stress. I work three jobs just to make enough money to pay the bills. The jobs aren't stressful, but worrying if I'm going to have enough money each month is. Running seems to be the only thing that clams my nerves.

Fletcher: I'm Fletcher . . .

Katie: . . . and I'm Katie . . .

Fletcher: . . . and the only way we can relieve our stress is by talking to each other.

Katie: My mother is very sick and she lives with us so I can take care of her.

Fletcher: And since Katie had to stop working to take care of her mother, I had to start working longer hours to make more money. Both of these things have put a lot of stress on us.

Katie: So, every night we take walk around our neighborhood and talk. The fresh air is wonderful and just being able to talk about our days and our future helps relax us both. We know that this situation is only temporary and as long as we have each other, we'll be able to survive.

CD, Track 26, Page 94

A. Listen to the phone conversation Mrs. Gregory is having with the doctor's office.

Receptionist: Good morning, Dr. Rosenberg's office.

Patient: Um, yes, this is Linda Gregory. I brought my daughter Courtney in a few weeks ago for her 6-month check-up. I just received the bill and I have a few questions.

Receptionist: Yes, Mrs. Gregory. Let me pull up your records. Do you have the date of the statement?

Patient: Yes, it is October 6th.

Receptionist: Ok, I have it right here. How can I help you?

Patient: Well, I don't see why I owe $20.

Receptionist: That is your co-pay.

Patient: But on the statement it says that I already paid my $20 co-pay

Receptionist: Yes, you're right. But when we talked to insurance company they told us that your co-pay is $40. You already paid $20, so you owe another $20.

Patient: $40? When did my co-pay go up to $40?

Receptionist: I don't know ma'am. You'll have to call your insurance company to find out.

Patient: Ok, so all I owe right now is $20?

Receptionist: Yes.

Patient: OK. Thank you for you time.

CD, Track 27, Page 95

C. Read and listen to the following conversation between a patient and the doctor's office.

Receptionist: Dr. Brook's office

Patient: Um, yes, this is Cooper Jackson. I came in and saw the doctor a few months ago for the pain I was having in my leg. I just received the bill and I have a few questions.

Receptionist: Of course, Mr. Jackson. Let me pull up your records. Do you have the date of the statement?

Patient: Yes, it is June 16th.

Receptionist: Ok, I have it here. How can I help you?

Patient: Well, I don't understand what this $264 charge is for.

Receptionist: That is for the X-rays the technician took of your leg.

Patient: OK, but shouldn't my insurance pay for that?

Receptionist: Yes, they might pay some. As you can see on the bill, we have billed your insurance company but are still waiting to hear back them. Once we do, we'll send you an adjusted bill reflecting how much you owe

Patient: Oh, so if I don't have to pay this $264, why did you send me a bill?

Receptionist: I know it may seem a bit confusing. Our billing department automatically sends out statements to our current patients every month, whether or not we have heard back from the insurance companies. It usually takes about a month for the bill to reflect what the insurance company has paid so, in general, if you wait two or three months to pay your bill, your statement should show the correct amount due.

Patient: I see. That makes sense. So, I don't need to pay this bill now?

Receptionist: No. Wait until you see an adjusted amount on there and then pay the bill.

Patient: Great! Thanks for your help.

Receptionist: Have a nice day, Mr. Jackson.

UNIT 6
CD, Track 28, Page 113, Exercise B

B. Listen to the conversation Maya is having with the salesperson. What does she want to know about the patio set? Write her questions below. Some questions are embedded.

Maya: Excuse me, could you answer some questions for me about the patio furniture?

Salesperson: Sure, which set are you looking at?

Maya: This teak set.

Salesperson: One of our best sellers. How can I help?

Maya: Well, I saw it online and was reading the reviews so I wanted to see what you thought.

Salesperson: Sure.

Maya: I want to know if it's comfortable.

Salesperson: Well, why don't you sit down and see for yourself?

Maya: Yeah, it is pretty comfortable. Is it lightweight, easy to move?

Salesperson: I think it's pretty lightweight for wood. Why don't you move the table a bit and see what you think?

Maya: Not bad. It's definitely lighter than it looks. How can I clean it?

Salesperson: A damp cloth should do just fine. And when the stain starts to fade, you can just get a brush and some teak oil to brighten it up again.

Maya: Oh, good. That was the next thing I was going to ask you. I've never owned teak before so I wasn't sure if it had to be re-sanded or what.

Salesperson: If you keep on top of it with the oil, it shouldn't need re-sanding.

Maya: Great. So, how does teak hold up in bad weather?

Salesperson: Just fine. The sun will cause the fading but we already talked about how to fix that. It's heavy enough that it won't get blown by wind. And it does just fine in the rain.

Maya: Good to know. So how much does this set, with the table, umbrella and four chairs cost?

Salesperson: $1,450.

Maya: And I got this 20% off coupon in the mail. Can I use it?

Salesperson: Sure. That will bring the price down to around $1,160.

Maya: OK. Oh and one more thing. Does it come with a warranty?

Salesperson: Yep, a 90-day manufacturers warranty against any product defects.

Maya: Great. I'll talk it over with my husband and then we'll make a decision. Thanks for your help.

Salesperson: No problem. That's what I'm here for!

CD, Track 29, Page 116

C. Listen to four phone conversations between salespeople and customers who are buying items from this catalog page. Complete the chart below based on what you hear.

Conversation 1

Salesperson: Cook-It-Right Catalog Sales. Would you like to order something from our catalog?

Customer: Yes, I'd like to order item number 925163-2.

Salesperson: How many?

Customer: Just one, please.

Salesperson: OK, your total will be $32.42 with tax. Will you be paying with Versa, MisterCard, or Discovery today?

Customer: Versa.

Salesperson: Great. I'll need the number and expiration date whenever you're ready.

Conversation 2

Salesperson: Cook-It-Right Catalog Sales. Would you like to order something from our catalog?

Customer: Yes, I'd like to order item number 986534-9.

Salesperson: How many?

Customer: Just one, please.

Salesperson: OK, your total will be $21.60. Will you be paying with Versa, MisterCard, or Discovery today?

Customer: You don't take American Expression?

Salesperson: Sorry, ma'am. No.

Customer: OK, I'll pay with Discovery.

Salesperson: Great. I'll need the number and expiration date whenever you're ready.

Conversation 3

Salesperson: Cook-It-Right Catalog Sales. Would you like to order something from our catalog?

Customer: Yes, I'd like to order item number 9132456-5.

Salesperson: How many?

Customer: Two, please.

Salesperson: OK, your total will be $205.57 with tax and shipping.

Will you be paying with Versa, MisterCard or Discovery today?
Customer: Discovery.
Salesperson: Great. I'll need the number and expiration date whenever you're ready.

Conversation 4
Salesperson: Cook-It-Right Catalog Sales. Would you like to order something from our catalog?
Customer: Yes, I'd like to order item number 9673652-4.
Salesperson: All three pieces?
Customer: Just the muffin pan, please.
Salesperson: OK, your total will be $14.02 with tax. Will you be paying with Versa, MisterCard, or Discovery today?
Customer: MisterCard.
Salesperson: Great. I'll need the number and expiration date whenever you're ready.

CD, Track 30, Page 122
B. Read and listen to the conversation.
Sales Associate: Can I help you with something?
Customer: Yes, I'd like to return these shoes. I wore them around my house on the carpet for a few days and they are still uncomfortable. The salesman who sold them to me insisted they would stretch out and soften up, but they haven't. I'd like to get my money back.
Sales Associate: I'm afraid I can't give you your money back. These were on sale and we don't offer refunds for sale items.
Customer: Can I exchange them?
Sales Associate: Yes, you can exchange them for something of equal value.
Customer: Ok, I'll do that. Let me look around for a bit.
Sales Associate: Take your time.

CD, Track 31, Page 122
C. Listen to each question and write the correct answer.
1. What is the customer trying to return?
2. Why is she returning them?
3. Will the store give her her money back?
4. Why not?
5. What does the sales associate say the customer can do?
6. Does the customer seem satisfied?

CD, Track 32, Page 124
Listen to six conversations and write the corresponding conversation number in front of the reason each person gave for returning the product. Then, write what product the person returned.

Conversation 1
Sales Associate: Can I help you with something?
Customer: Yes, I'd like to exchange this phone for a different one.
Sales Associate: Is something wrong with it?
Customer: Well, I can't hear the person on the other end very well when I'm at my house or at work. Basically, that makes the phone useless to me.
Sales Associate: Yeah that's not good. Let's get you another one and see if it works better.
Customer: Thanks.

Conversation 2
Sales Associate: How can I help you?
Customer: I bought these pants here last week and I didn't have time to try them on. When I got home and put them on, I realized they are too small. Can I try on a larger size?
Sales Associate: Let me see if we have them in stock. You're in luck! Here, let me get you a fitting room.

Conversation 3
Sales Associate: Can I help you with something?
Customer: Yes, I ordered these glasses online and when I received

them in the mail, they were all broken. I thought it would be easier to return them to the store rather than trying to ship them back.
Sales Associate: Good idea. Unfortunately, we are all out of these right now. Would you like me to give you a credit and then we'll call you when they come in?
Customer: Could I get something different?
Sales Associate: Certainly. Why don't you look around and I'll hold them up here at the counter for you.
Customer: Great.

Conversation 4
Sales Associate: What can I do for you today?
Customer: Well, I got this printer home and realized it doesn't work with my computer. I called tech support and they told me I never should've been sold this printer because it doesn't come with a driver to make it work with my computer.
Sales Associate: I'm sorry about that. Would you like to shop around for another printer?
Customer: No, I think I just want my money back.
Sales Associate: As long as you have your receipt, we can definitely do that.
Customer: Here it is.

Conversation 5
Customer: Hi. I need to exchange these diapers for a larger size. I accidentally bought the wrong ones.
Sales Associate: No worries. Why don't you go ahead and pick out the size you need and come back and I'll do the exchange for you.
Customer: Perfect. Thanks!

Conversation 6
Sales Associate: Can I help you with something?
Customer: Yes, I was given these three books last week and I actually already own them.
Sales Associate: Do you have a receipt?
Customer: I don't
Sales Associate: OK, well let me see how much they were and then you can exchange them for something of equal value.
Customer: Sounds great. Thank you.

UNIT 7
CD, Track 33, Page 139
E. Listen to the conversations between employees at a small printing company. Write the problems and the suggestions for fixing them in the chart below.
Conversation 1
Aaron: Hey, Linda, could you help me for a second?
Linda: Sure. What do you need?
Aaron: Something is wrong with my printer. The pages are coming out faded and splotchy.
Linda: Hmm. Sounds like a problem with your toner. Did you take it out and shake it?
Aaron: I tried that. It didn't help.
Linda: Well then, you probably need to replace the cartridge. When is the last time you changed it?
Aaron: I have no idea. Maybe six months ago?
Linda: Yep, that's probably the issue. Put another one in and see if that helps.
Aaron: Thanks, Linda.

Conversation 2
Preston: Oh, Mark, I'm so glad you were walking by.
Mark: What's up?
Preston: For some reason, my computer won't turn on.
Mark: That's strange.
Preston: I know. It was working just fine before lunch.
Mark: Did you check to make sure the power cord is plugged in?
Preston: No. Let me check. Boy, do I feel stupid. I must have knocked it out with my foot.

Mark: Happens to the best of us.
Preston: Thanks.

Conversation 3
Kim: Claudia, do you know anything about this photocopier?
Claudia: I know a bit. Try me.
Kim: Well, it's just not working. When I push the green button, nothing happens.
Claudia: Is it plugged in?
Kim: Yep.
Claudia: Did you check to make sure there is paper in the paper tray?
Kim: Yep, it has plenty.
Claudia: What about the toner?
Kim: I didn't check the toner. How do I do that?
Claudia: Well, you can see on the display right here how much toner is left in the cartridge. Yep, it looks like it's low. This copier won't even try to make copies if the toner is too low. If you put a new toner cartridge in, that should solve your problem.
Kim: Thanks, Claudia.

UNIT 8
CD, Track 34, Page 159
E. Listen to the immigration officer talk about how to become a citizen. Fill in the missing words.
United States (U.S.) citizenship carries many responsibilities with it. The decision to become a U.S. citizen is a very important one. Being granted U.S. citizenship is known as naturalization. In most cases, a person who wants to naturalize must first be a permanent resident. By becoming a U.S. citizen, you gain many rights that permanent residents or others do not have, including the right to vote. To be eligible for naturalization, you must first meet certain requirements set by U.S. law.

What are the basic requirements to apply for naturalization?
Generally, to be eligible for naturalization you must:
- Be age 18 or older; and
- Be a permanent resident for a certain amount of time (usually 5 years); and
- Be a person of good moral character; and
- Have a basic knowledge of U.S. history and government; and
- Have a period of continuous residence and physical presence in the U.S.; and
- Be able to read, write and speak basic English. There are exceptions to this rule for someone who:
- Is 55 years old and has been a permanent resident for at least 15 years; or
- Is 50 years old and has been a permanent resident for at least 20 years; or
- Has a physical or mental impairment that makes them unable to fulfill these requirements.

When can I apply for naturalization?
You may be able to apply for naturalization if you are at least 18 years of age and have been a permanent resident of the U.S.:
- For at least 5 years; or
- For at least 3 years during which time you have been, and continue to be, married to and living in marriage with your U.S. citizen husband or wife; or
- Have honorable service in the U.S. military. Certain spouses of U.S. citizens and members of the military may be able to file for naturalization sooner than noted above previously.

Skills Index

ACADEMIC SKILLS

Brainstorming, 48, 71, 81, 100, 125, 153, 169, 171

Calculations
Annual and monthly expenses, 26
Gas mileage and cost per mile, 56, 57, 58, 62

Categorizing, P5, 18, 67, 75, 156, 166

Charts, graphs, and diagrams, P1, P5, 7, 17, 30, 48, 56, 58, 60, 65, 67, 69, 70, 79, 82, 89, 97, 99, 107, 116, 134, 139, 140, 156, 171

Drawing, 134, 141

Editing, P8, 11, 129

Estimating costs, 78

Grammar
Adverb clauses of concession, 102
Appositives, 126, 129
Causative verbs, 70, 71, 77, 84
Dependent clauses, 102
Future perfect tense, 17, 19
Independent clauses, 102
Noun and verb forms, 68
Noun clauses, 148, 149
Parts of speech, 152
Past perfect continuous tense, 30
Past perfect progressive tense, 40–41
Simple past tense, 40–41
Simple tenses, 10
Transitional expressions, 171
Word families, 89, 134

Group activities, P5, P6, P8, 5, 7, 12, 15, 23, 27, 31, 34, 37, 39, 44, 46, 47, 48, 50, 53, 58, 59, 61, 72, 73, 76, 78, 81, 91, 97, 99, 101, 102, 103, 113, 115, 116, 117, 118, 122, 127, 128, 138, 140, 141, 143, 148, 153, 160, 162, 165, 168, 169, 175

Learning styles, 3–5

Listening
Conversations, P1, P2, P3, 8, 15, 29, 56, 69, 94, 95, 113, 116, 122, 124, 139
Descriptions, 9
Discussion, 7, 37, 48, 78, 83, 91
Explanations, 159
Interviews, 38
Introductions, P3
Lectures, 3, 13, 25
Questions, 122
Sales pitches, 47

Matching, 5, 6, 42, 54, 64, 68, 70, 100, 124, 130, 136, 139, 142, 161

Multiple-choice questions, 38, 55, 121, 140, 150

Partner activities, P2, P3, 4, 6, 8, 9, 10, 11, 14, 15, 17, 25, 28, 32, 36, 49, 50, 51, 54, 62, 65, 69, 71, 74, 75, 77, 84, 86, 95, 96, 97, 100, 105, 106, 119, 121, 125, 128, 129, 130, 135, 137, 144, 158, 159, 163, 166, 168, 169, 173

Prioritizing, 14

Reading
Ads, 28, 125
Articles, 4, 31–32, 34–36, 144–146
Bill of Rights, 160, 161, 162
Catalogs, 116, 128
Charts and graphs, 7, 17, 30, 48, 70, 97, 98, 102, 105, 107, 148
Conversations, P2, 56, 69, 95, 122
Descriptions, 143, 157, 161, 163, 164, 165
Doctor's bills, 96, 106
E-mail messages, P7, P9
Fliers, 12
Instruction manuals, 135, 137, 138, 139, 150
Insurance policies, 53, 63, 79, 85
Introductions, P3
Lists, 23, 27, 31, 71, 75, 101, 114
Main ideas, 34–36
Maintenance and repair guides, 51, 52
Newsletters, 81, 82
Newspaper columns, 92, 93
Noun and verb forms, 68
Paragraphs, 10
Personal letters, P7
Phrases, 64
Plan for carpooling, 167
Product reviews, 114, 115
Rental agreements, 72, 73, 74
Report guidelines, 147
Reports, 147
Research data, 60
Return policies, 123
Scenarios, 41, 54
Sentences, 24, 155, 156
Statements, 16, 53, 101, 126
Tables, 99
Thank-you notes, P8
Warranties and guarantees, 76, 119, 120, 121, 129
Web sites, 29, 44, 117, 158
Worksheets, 26

Research strategies, P10, 21, 43, 48, 65, 87, 109, 118, 131, 153, 175

Selecting responses, 16, 29, 61, 126, 172

Speaking
Answering questions, 8, 10, 86, 105
Asking questions, P6, 8, 11, 19, 49, 86, 97, 115, 128, 129
Conversations, 69, 71, 84, 95, 96, 106, 118
Discussion, P6, 1, 4, 5, 6, 7, 9, 12, 14, 15, 17, 23, 25, 27, 31, 32, 34, 37, 44, 46, 47, 50, 53, 58, 61, 62, 72, 73, 76, 78, 91, 97, 101, 103, 113, 115, 117, 122, 138, 141, 158, 159, 162
Expressing opinions, 169
Instructions, 135
Interviewing, 18, 99, 166
Introductions, P1, P2, P3
Presentations, P6, 37, 61, 73, 127, 140, 175
Sharing with partner, P3

Spelling, 68

Team projects, 22, 44, 66, 88, 110, 132, 154, 176

True/false questions, 29, 86

Vocabulary
Addiction, 100, 108
Balancing your life, 1–2
Careers, 1–2, 6, 20
Cars, 45–46, 50, 64
Civic responsibility, 155–156, 174
Dictionary use, 2, 23, 36, 50, 67, 68, 81, 89–90, 111, 112
Finances, 23–24, 42
First aid, 103–104
Guessing meanings of words, 155
Health, 89–90, 108
Housing, 67–68, 86
Idioms, 23
Learning styles, 1–2
Motivation, 1–2
Office, 133–134, 152
Retail sales, 111–112
Synonyms, 112

Writing
Ads, 127
Alphabetical order, 142, 151
Answers to questions, P3, 11, 12, 13, 25, 28, 39, 41, 51, 60, 63, 70, 80, 81, 85, 90, 93, 94, 107, 115, 118, 119, 122, 127, 128, 138, 144, 151, 163, 164, 165, 170
Bill of Rights, 162
Categorizing, P5
Charts, graphs, and diagrams, P1, 56, 58, 65, 67, 69, 79, 82, 89, 99, 116, 134, 139, 140, 156, 171

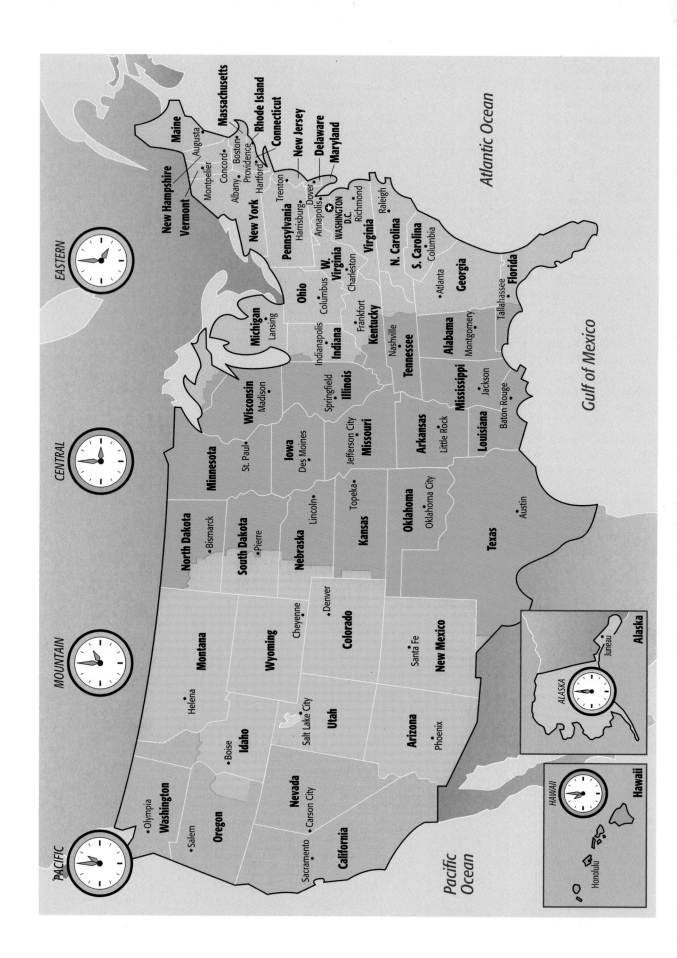